Fighting Lions with Loo Rolls

An African Experience

Kathleen Rigby

ISBN# 978-9966-757-61-6

Old Africa Books
PO Box 2338
Naivasha, Kenya 20117

Praise for Fighting Lions with Loo Rolls

first met Kathy about 30 years ago, when she had recently moved back to the USA from Kenya. We would walk around a local lake, and she made strange comments! We would watch a flock of geese landing on the water and she would say, "But where are the hippos?" I would ask her how her morning was going and she would say, "Oh, how I miss the sound of lions roaring in the early morning!" We listened to the sound of traffic roaring nearby! It was hard for me to relate to how much she missed her adopted home, her Kenya.

Kathy told me many tales over the years, of amazing safaris, of lions and elephants, snakes and scorpions, of her research and her singing career, of the wonderful community of talented, fascinating people, of her motorcycle accident and her long recovery. However, until I read her incredible book, I had never really understood how colorful, uplifting, dangerous, exhilarating and close to Nature her years in Kenya had been. Each story is another adventure, and from the safety of my living room couch, it is an exciting and page-turning read!

For those who share Kathy's love of Kenya, this memoir will remind them of the joys and challenges, the thrills and the fears of their lives there. For those like me who have always wanted to go to Africa, it is an intense way to experience it through her eyes, and to read how amazing life was for ex-pats in Africa 30 years ago. Reading the stories of this courageous and dedicated woman, a loving mother and her adventurous family, renews my life-long desire to go on a Safari and see the migrations, the Serengeti, the Maasai culture, and the wildness and beauty that is Kenya.

- Juliet Millard, PhD

Contents

Acknowledgments

It is with robust enthusiasm that I thank Peggy Davis, the Life Style Director at the Grande Dunes Ocean Club in Myrtle Beach, South Carolina. When I first talked with Peggy about my life, she said, "If only you had a book." Her support, encouragement and belief in me were so strong that I went home and immediately set to work to finish the book. I had about one-third of the book written at that time. Peggy is one of those motivating helpers that fortunate people are given in this life to encourage them. After talking with her, I knew THIS was the time I was supposed to finish writing our story. Thank you for believing in me, Peggy.

Thanks to my beloved husband, Hugh, for providing the wild ride and bold experiences in the book. Thanks also for your stories, your dedication and caring for our family and others in this world, for your support, your avant garde thinking, your astute taking and archiving of our family photographs.

Thanks to Rachel and Zak for enduring unique childhood experiences, and for accepting your "unusual" parents. Thank you too for loving your Kenyan experiences. It is to both of you, and your beautiful children, that I dedicate this book – for them to know our family's story.

Thanks to Mom for keeping my letters during the decades I was overseas. And for passing along her love of books to me. She even had a story of her own published in her youth.

Thank you to all the many fabulous people mentioned inside of these pages – definite characters all. Days in Kenya would have been boring without you. I love every one of you for your uniqueness, for our vivid shared experiences, for being our friends, for the adventures we shared and for all the ways in which you enriched our lives.

Thank you Mike and Jan McCoy for giving us our first Old Africa Magazine when we were staying with you several years ago. It was the start of this literary journey.

Thanks to the wonderful Editor of Old Africa Magazine and

Books, Shel Arensen, and his son Blake, for pointing me in their direction when I was looking for a publisher. I am eternally grateful for making this process as painless as possible, guiding me from stories to a book. It has been a wonderful experience. Thanks also for keeping East African history alive.

To my dear friend, Jule, for your input of constructive ideas as well as decades of true friendship.

To Esmond Bradley Martin, Joan Root, George and Joy Adamson – all brave wildlife warriors who should never have died in such brutal and thankless ways; and to Daphne Sheldrick, Tony Fitzjohn, Richard Leakey and Kuki Gallman, who have tried so hard to preserve Africa's beautiful animals. You are my heroes and heroines in the conservation struggle.

Lastly, thank you Kenya and Africa – for your beauty, your wildlife, your secrets, your ancient ways, your people, your intrigue, your unique character and for your very existence. May it be forever.

Foreword

We all miss the Good Ol' Days, when we were young and every morning promised new adventure. We each have our own good ol' days, and in this marvelous memoir Kathy Rigby relives the exuberant youth experienced by those of us with the great fortune of living in post-independence Kenya, a time when East Africa hovered between the short period of British colonialism, with its remarkable combination of Edwardian gentility and ferocious primeval splendor, and today's booming, overcrowded modernity hurtling toward Malthusian meltdown.

Kathy beautifully recaptures the courage and eccentricity of the White Kenyans and young western expats who comprised our social scene; nearly all were accomplished, many were brilliant, none were dull. She evokes the excitement of safari, the sagging Land Rover piled high with tents, bedding, food, and water, spare tires and fuel, a Hilift jack, spare suspension parts and a full set of tools, friends, children and babies, heading to a campsite in Tsavo or the Mara or the arid wilds of the NFD (Northern Frontier District), where endless miles of corrugations rattled the car, contents, and passengers to pieces. The land felt endless and empty, but just drop your trousers behind a thorn bush and a curious crowd would materialize. Vultures and eagles still dotted the skies, abundant wildlife still grazed the dry grass and browsed the thorn bush, and lions, hyenas, and zebras still sang around impromptu roadside campsites at night.

By the late twentieth century we may have missed the full riotous abundance of nature and prodigious cultural diversity of precolonial primeval Africa but our lives were forever shaped and enriched by that which remained. It was a magical time and place to be young, and like all such times and places, it exists only in memory. I am deeply grateful to Kathy Rigby for so beautifully capturing the essence of those formative years, reviving memories that were sinking into the sediments of old age, and inspiring today's young people to seek adventure and wisdom in the world's remaining wilderness.

- Dr Laurence Frank, Berkeley, California

It was the dead of night, and it was black. The wind howled intensely, swirling the blizzard of snow that was falling down hard outside my bedroom window. In my twilight of gradual wakening, the roaring wind was the roaring lions I was used to hearing outside my bedroom windows, and I was back in Kenya. As I gradually woke and realized I was no longer there, and the lions I loved and missed were the howling winds of freezing Upstate NY, the place of my birth, my heart sank as the reality of leaving Kenya hit home.

Introduction
The Man on the Train –
A Shadow of Things to Come

In the mirror of my memory, I recall seeing him sitting on the London underground in 1975. As a young woman who had lived in four other countries by age 20, I had seen many different kinds of people. But I had never seen anyone who looked like him.

His exotic differentness struck me. His bearing was poised and dignified, almost regal. His flowing, indigo blue patterned kaftan with ornamental embroidery made me think he came from West Africa. His rich gold jewelry against his dark skin made him look elegant and extraordinary. I could not turn away or keep from staring. His teeth had been filed to points, and he had facial scars in a pattern so precise and perfect in the placement of every raised lump, designed to make him look fierce - like a leopard. I sat in awe!

Such body modification in his society would give non-verbal messages to others. It might identify the tribe or culture he belonged to or tell of his status within the tribe. In some societies it might have been a rite of passage performed during the transition from childhood to adolescence, granting admittance to the adult tribal community. In several parts of East Africa, 'slayer' scars told of successful hunting – even of humans. Killing an enemy allowed the fortunate huntsman to decorate himself with keloidal scars on the forehead, cheeks, shoulders and upper arms.

My heart thumped as I sat down next to him on the underground train. I confess, I was intimidated by his frightening looks - his filed teeth and facial scars. Yet, he sat ramrod straight, tall and dignified, strong and proud and motionless, looking straight ahead. I wished I could talk with him. What stories he could tell, I thought.

Despite this encounter on the underground, nothing in my early life indicated I would ever go to Africa, let alone live there. Little did I know what the future held in store for me and my family.

Chapter One
Before Coming to Kenya

Hugh and I met in Toronto, Canada, where we had both emigrated to. I came from Rochester, New York, on the other side of Lake Ontario from Toronto. A failed romance led me to conclude that Rochester was too small a city for me to remain in. So, at age 18, I left family, friends and home and moved to Toronto, with hardly a penny to my name. Within three days I had a great job as a fashion clothing designer in the 'Village' and had met the amazing young man I was to marry.

By the age of 21, Hugh had already explored India, Afghanistan, Pakistan, Greece, Turkey, most of Europe, the Scandinavian countries and many other places. He decided it was time to see Canada and North America - where he met me. We saved some money and started travelling. On Oahu in Hawaii, we married and lived for six months. When I became pregnant, we moved to Hugh's homeland of Cheshire, England. Hugh wanted to work in forestry, so we decided to move to the beautiful, but very remote Loch Awe in the Highlands of Scotland where he had gotten a job with the Forestry Commission. Coincidentally, Hugh's Grandmother lived about one hour away, near Crinan Canal, in Duntrune Castle.

Hugh went before me to find a home for us. I stayed with Hugh's parents for a fortnight before I left to start life in the Highlands of Scotland. I was now eight months pregnant. I carried a suitcase in one hand, a cat in a cage in the other and a rabbit in a cage under my arm, as I boarded the train which would eventually end at the remote Taynuilt Station in the Western Highlands. I had to change stations in Glasgow where I disembarked. The next one was on Sauchiehall Street only a few blocks away, but when I asked directions, I could not understand a single word any one was telling me. The beautiful, sing song lilt and Gaelic linguistic heritage makes the Glaswegian accent a strong one, which my ears were unaccustomed to. They also speak their own language. For example, "Ge ut mi road, lass," (in my language means) "Get out of my way, girl." "I dunna ken," means I do not know. Many words were different, and the accent was strong and different to what I knew. It takes some getting used to. When I asked for directions, my confusion obviously showed. In the end, two nice young men took my cases from me and walked me over to the next station, where I embarked on the next leg of my journey.

I had been in transit for many long hours with no food or drink, but my journey continued. It soon grew dark as we ascended the mountains, and I could see nothing of the beauty of our new home in the Western Highlands. It was pitch black at 11 pm when I finally reached the remote platform at Taynuilt. By this time, I was only one of three passengers left on the train, and now I was the only passenger getting off at Taynuilt. The station was closed and locked up. All lights were off except for one on the platform. Now, I was the only person - heavily pregnant - alone in the dark forest that surrounded the station in the middle of the night. It was not a comforting situation. Hugh was nowhere to be seen in the darkness and stillness that enveloped me as the train pulled away and was swallowed up by the night. There was no way to telephone Hugh; there were no cell phones in those days. Our home didn't even have one, which was the norm in Scotland then. I told myself Hugh would be along soon and settled down on the bench, where I listened to the night noises coming from the dark forest. I wondered if there were bears, wolves, or other predators. Time passed slowly. After more than one hour, I at last heard the sound of a car approaching. Hugh had purchased a 1935 Austin A35 for our use. It was ancient, on its last legs, and all we could afford. It had refused to start when he had set out for the hour-long drive to come and get me via the twisty, one-laned road over the mountains, with sheer drops off the side, in the dark night. I felt enormous relief at the long-awaited sight of him! Thus began our lives in Scotland.

Our daughter, Rachel, was born in the small, seaside town of Oban, on the dark blue waters of the Firth of Lorn, which overlooks the Islands of Mull, Kerrera, and Lismore. In those days, the long-haired, long-horned Highland cattle were still driven through the main streets of the town, holding up traffic. Oban was that small a place. The pregnant women from the Highlands and the Islands came to a home in Oban to have their babies with the help of a couple of midwives. The doctor came once a month. Women who were close to their birthing time, gathered. The doctor gave us hormone pills that were meant to bring on labor so there could be a doctor present for the births. One by one, the women had their babies. Only I remained without so much as a contraction. Three days later my labor finally began. As there was now no doctor in the town, and the two midwives were extremely busy caring for the other women who had delivered, and their babies, I gave birth to my first-born child sitting up in a chair, alone – without any pain-relieving medicines. Husbands were not allowed to be present. There was no such thing as birthing classes. I knew nothing of what to expect and had no family or friends with whom to talk of such things.

We named our daughter Rachel, which means a ewe (female)

Our house (the right half) and car on Loch Awe, Argyll, Scotland.

lamb, because of the many times we had to stop the car and wait for a sheep to give birth on the narrow single-lane road with deadly drops off the side of the mountain, on our way into Oban, for me to give birth. It seemed a very fitting name.

After a couple years of living in the middle of the forest on the side of Loch Awe, we changed plans and moved to Manchester, England, for Hugh to get a degree in Three Dimensional Design at Art College. Our son Zachary was born there. After getting a Master's Degree in Teaching and spending a decade in the UK, we moved back to the United States to be near my family. But after a couple of difficult years there, we got another chance to move to Kenya.

Both Hugh and I wanted to use our lives and our energy to do something meaningful. It may sound corny, but we wanted, in whatever humble way possible, to use our energies to help those less fortunate or more vulnerable than ourselves. We wanted our lives to have a purpose. After all, we were children of the 1960s – a time when thoughts of Karma and seeking higher knowledge through meditation practices was an alternative to organized religion, a time when people sought peace and love, and a desire to change the world to be a better place. It was a time of high idealism in the Western world. We agreed with those sentiments.

We cared about animals as well, recognizing their right to live on this earth too, and we saw clearly how much they enriched our lives and our world. When we had the chance to move to Kenya, we thought that being around the great abundance of animal life in Africa would be wondrous and awe-inspiring and would connect us with the base of life, like our earlier ancestors, putting our very beings in perspective.

Deciding to come to Kenya was a story in itself. When Hugh was finishing his Master's Degree in Education in England, he received a copy of the Old Rugbeian newsletter. In it was an article from the Headmaster of the Banda School in Nairobi, Dougie Dalrymple, who was also an old Rugbeian. Hugh and his brothers were graduates of Rugby - a famous, but tough English boarding school. Dougie said if any old Rugbeians, (graduates of Rugby School) came to Kenya to visit, they should come to the Banda School and introduce themselves. Hugh immediately wrote to ask if they needed an additional teacher with his background. Unknown to us, his younger brother Stephen, who was then living in the South of England, had also read the same article and had written to Dougie Dalrymple too, also asking for a teaching position. Stephen had experience teaching in Africa. He went to college in South Africa and then taught in Rhodesia. He was hired as the Deputy Head Master for Banda School, and he and his wife, Sally, went to live in Kenya. There had not been a job for Hugh at that time, so we moved to America, back to my hometown of Rochester, New York. But after a harrowing two years in America where Rachel faced the deadly illness of cancer (leukemia) and Zak had meningitis that would not leave him for the first year of his life, a place opened up at the Banda School. We left America and joined Stephen and Sally at the Banda School, outside of Nairobi, Kenya.

Banda means hut. The Banda School started its life as the Banda Hotel - originally a small inn outside of Nairobi, along the Magadi Road. In the Swahili, Indian and Malayan cultures, *banda* refers to a building of mud and wattle with a rough *makuti* roof. *Makuti* is thatching made from the sun-dried leaves of the coconut palm and is widely used across East Africa. The original owners and developers of the school, Mr. and Mrs. James Chitty, decided to name their school after the former Banda Hotel.

A lot of effort went into putting up this international school's infrastructure while peacefully co-existing with the wildlife. In Jim Chitty's words, "It was not uncommon to see giraffe grazing off the bushes, families of warthogs taking their evening stroll and lions gazing curiously where children now wait for the bus." The shoulder high grass was cut even as the workers, mostly women, shrieked every time they discovered one deadly poisonous puff adder snake after another. Classes were put up, playing fields were levelled, and the swimming pool hole was excavated.

The Banda School officially opened its doors to 24 children with eight teaching staff and a Headmaster in September 1966. Today, it is among the best international schools in Kenya, and is in line with modern British Preparatory Schools in the United Kingdom. (https://www.bandaschool.com/375/history)

It was a unique and vibrant school with a wonderfully positive atmosphere. Pupils and teachers at the Banda exhibited a great

Rachel and Zachary walking to the Banda school (in the background) in their uniforms.

deal of mutual respect, alongside a shared sense of fun and a desire to succeed. The teaching staff invested in ensuring that every child in their care would strive to achieve his or her best, including extracurricular activities, making the Banda one of the best schools in Kenya. Hugh was so happy to be teaching in his own respectful culture again.

Living in Kenya turned our lives into an exciting adventure, filled with new experiences. Not all were good. The first weekend there, we left the kids with our sister-in-law, Sally, and went into Nairobi to get money from the bank and to buy groceries for the week. I waited in the old Renault car that Hugh had purchased from a teacher who was leaving the country while Hugh went to the bank to get money. It took longer than I expected. When Hugh did finally make his way back to the car, he told me that after he had made his withdrawal and left the bank, he had been overwhelmed by four men right on the main street. They had surrounded him and relieved him of his money and his unused traveler's checks. The traveler's checks were later cashed at the bank with signatures that did not in any way resemble Hugh's – indicating an inside job. This was our introduction to the dangers of Kenya with risk every minute of every day. But I've jumped ahead in my story.

Chapter Two
Primed and Prepped to live in the Colonies

I fearfully led my two children, Rachel age 7, and Zachary age 4, onto a plane in 1979 to start a new life in Kenya, East Africa. My husband Hugh would be teaching at a British Preparatory School known as the Banda School. Nothing in my early life indicated I would ever live in Africa. With no knowledge of life there, my anticipation was large.

By contrast, everything about my husband, his family and upbringing had prepared him for a life abroad. Though Hugh was born in England in the post-colonial era, his family had lived, settled and worked in many countries around the world for generations.

At its height in the 19th and 20th century, Great Britain controlled territory larger than any other empire in history, leading to the statement: "The sun never sets on the British Empire."

Hugh's mother's family settled in Madeira in the 1700s. They established wineries and embroidery factories on the Island, which served the colonies of the British Empire. Hugh's great-great-great-grandfather founded the Rigby Rifle factory in Dublin, Ireland (William and James Rigby Company) in 1735. It is still in business today, though not still in the Rigby family. Hugh's great-grandfather moved to England from Ireland to run the Royal Armoury at Enfield. His son, Dr. Hugh Mallinson Rigby, became a Harley Street Specialist and King George V's surgeon. He was knighted for saving the King's life, becoming Sir Hugh Rigby.

Hugh's grandmother, Muriel Hobhouse Malcolm, was awarded the British Empire Medal (BEM) in 1946 for meritorious civil/military service, worthy of recognition by the Crown, for running the Arms Services Club in London during the height of the German bombing during World War II. She was also the first woman pilot to fly her own plane across the English Channel after the war.

Hugh's father, Sir John Rigby, had been Earl Mountbatten of Burma's 'right-hand man' - the British Government's Representative in Delhi, India, during the India/Pakistan Partition. Working under Prime Minister Winston Churchill, he had also been one of the masterminds behind the movement of troops and supplies across the English Channel from Britain to the D-Day landings on the Normandy beaches of France. He had an astounding memory and could quote train schedules for any train in India during the time he worked on such logistical issues ten years earlier. He could recall the movements the troops depended on for D-Day. He was a bit of a genius in that way. Because he had such an extremely precise mind, it drove him to distraction if tea was not served at exactly 4 pm on the dot!

Hugh's Uncle Roger was stationed in the Khyber Pass of Pakistan in WWII in the 1940s. Another relative, Sir Derek Erskine, settled in Kenya at the end of the First World War. He encouraged Kenyan runners, together with Archie Evans, building the foundation for the country's successful Olympic teams in later years. Derek contributed significant funds to athletics and donated the land on which the Nyayo National Stadium is now built. He was knighted for his contributions. He and his wife, Elizabeth, also started Erskine and Price Foods and raised their family in Kenya.

Hugh's brother, Anthony, had been a teacher in the Punjab of India, while his brother Stephen, was teaching in Rhodesia when he was only 17. His brother Jamie lived and worked in South Africa. Hugh himself traveled the Silk Road across Turkey, Iran, Pakistan and India before he was 20 years old. Because of his Spartan-like experience in boarding school, where deprivation of comfort of any kind was deemed the best preparation for serving the Empire in remote and difficult places, he managed to live in India for an entire year on less than £100 by sleeping under bushes. He had explored and experienced the world before I met him when he was the ripe old age of 21.

Hugh and I met in Toronto, Canada, in 1969 after I had left a small city in upstate New York, following a failed romance. He had emigrated from England. I was 18 and I met Hugh the morning after I moved to Toronto, waiting in line to use the washroom in a large house where the occupants of the rooms shared one bathroom. While we waited to use the facility, we started talking. Things moved quickly after that. I got a job as a clothing designer in a large store in 'The Village' where rock groups played and commissioned clothing that I designed. Three months later we were married.

Chapter Three
The Long Night's Journey

Looking back, I now see that the tone of the next ten years of our lives began with the tumultuous journey to Kenya in 1979. It was not a smooth transition. While enroute from the United States, we had stopped in England to visit my husband's family and to attend the weddings of two of his brothers. Then Hugh had left for Kenya to get things ready for our new lives there. The children and I stayed on in England. The night before departure, while staying with friends in Manchester, my young son fell and broke his arm between the wrist and the elbow. In true British stiff-upper-lip fashion, my friend told me not to mollycoddle Zak when I said I was taking him to the hospital. With a mothers' x-ray vision, I could see the bone projecting forward under the skin. In truth, I had always been able to read the unreadable illnesses of my son, like the deadly spinal meningitis that I saw coming for several weeks before the doctors could. The disease kept our three-week-old infant son away from us for most of his first year of life, and nearly took his life.

I called for a taxi to drive us to the hospital, where we waited through the night until they finished setting his little arm in a cast. We arrived back to waken my sleeping daughter, Rachel, just in time to catch our early morning flight to Kenya after our sleepless night. The plane had a number of young and eager British teachers making their way to various schools around Kenya. They soon formed a caring group around my children, reading to them, making them comfortable and occupying their attention.

The plane touched down in Egypt, where we were to change planes. Guards with machine guns trained on us watched as we filed out and walked along the runway to an official behind a desk. He took our passports mumbling things about how the United States was an ally of the Jewish people. I had never considered the politics of the region. I soon realized that in the eyes of the Egyptian officials, our passports made us somehow personally responsible for the foreign policy between the United States and Israel and Egypt.

The Egyptian officials kept our passports and led us to a little room where we sat on hard, upright chairs for long hours through the night, waiting and wondering what was happening. They locked the door behind us. I drew some small comfort from the fact that a few of the young British teachers were also locked in the room with us. In my concern, I ran through my limited knowledge of US relations with Egypt. Why were we being detained without our passports in this small room? I later found out that US support for Israel in the 1967 Six Day War made US passport holders suspect.

As I looked at my two young children huddling in the corner, sitting on rock hard upright chairs through another long sleepless night in this stark and uncomfortable room, with bright lights glaring in our eyes, I wondered what would become of us. What had we gotten them into – poor innocent children? I had never been entirely comfortable with this move. In fact, I had fought bitterly against it out of concern for my children. I had wanted to stay near my family and friends in upstate New York. It had taken a whole decade of living in England to convince my British husband to move to my homeland. And now we had left it. I was deeply concerned for the health and safety of my children. Hugh, much more comfortable and knowledgeable about the world, didn't share my fears. But he wasn't here with us now.

As we sat locked in a room at the Egyptian airport, I reviewed the reasons why we had come to be sitting here. The timing had been right for Hugh to persuade me that a move to Africa would be a good thing. The year we had spent in the United States had been harrowing and filled with troubles. Hugh was ready to leave. Rachel had been diagnosed with leukemia within six months of our arrival in the US, but the illness was thankfully now in remission. The inner-city school in which Hugh had only recently started teaching, had closed – leaving him unemployed and without medical benefits for our family. And we had just bought a house three months earlier. Hugh wanted out.

After hours in the locked room, a military guard came and escorted us out of the room with no explanation. We made our way to our next flight. I carried little Zak, with his arm in a cast,

Zachary with his broken arm in a sling on his arrival in Kenya.

on my hip, with young Rachel in tow, holding my hand. In my other hand, I carried a boom box to bring music into our new lives and a bag which held four tin plates, four tin cups, four forks, four knives and four spoons, together with a few extra clothes for the children. They were all the possessions we had to begin our lives in a new world. I clutched tightly onto each of them.

Chapter Four
Life in the Mews

As our plane touched down at Jomo Kenyatta International Airport, we peered out the windows to see dry, flat plains with tall, brown, burnt-out grasses waving on top of red-blood earth. I remember through my sleepy haze, an overcast sky - the tiny airport standing alone on a vast plain with nothing at all around it. Not knowing the lay of the land or the seasons of Kenya, I didn't see the colorful beauty or wild animals roaming unhindered that I'd observed in pictures, and I wondered if we had gone to the right country.

It was good to see my husband standing on the other side of the immigration officials as we arrived at the airport in Embakasi on the outskirts of Nairobi. I was glad to unburden some of the responsibility for the children's safety onto his broad shoulders, especially as I had not been able to protect my son from injury. Exhausted and broken, we passed through the gates that opened to our new lives, our little family together again, after our long and fretful journey.

As we drove to our new home, my eyes were on stalks as we passed rows of galvanized tin-roofed, open stalls lining the roadside. They sold vegetables, exotic fruits, and items for everyday use. Gaily colored *khanga* sarongs blew in the wind in front of many kiosks. Every Kenyan woman wore the colorful khangas and used them for every need imaginable. Throngs of people walked along the crowded roadsides, carrying the every-day items they needed. We passed a housing estate, an airstrip, which I later came to know as Wilson Airport, and a Kenyan Army barracks on our way to Langata. Further down the road, only a small space between the trees marked the turning to the Mews - a renovated stable that had been made into five, connected, little housing units around a small, common square in the middle. The narrow, unpaved road was a vibrant red earth, with bright tropical vegetation lining its sides.

The brilliant tropical colors made a vivid impression and appealed to my eyes. Violet blue jacaranda trees, glorious in full bloom, captured my attention with their beauty. Purple bougainvillea, red hibiscus, orange flame and trumpet vines on roof tops, exploded with color. Frangipani blossoms scented the air and mixed with the smell of dust from the red road. Numerous brilliantly colored birds buzzed around, darting in and out of the bushes singing their cheerful songs. The scene was almost aggressively beautiful in its strong, striking, amazingly sharp colors.

African people traversed this red road, barefoot, wearing brightly colored garb, on their way to their villages. Women often carried huge loads of firewood by a strap across their foreheads, or large buckets of water on top of their heads. Men usually carried *pangas* (machetes) – an all-purpose tool used for their days' work of toiling in a garden or for cutting things. All of the different sights and smells were totally foreign to anything we had ever seen before and set our senses swinging.

Our car turned into the circular drive that lined the common square of earth in front of the houses. Our new dwelling smelled of dampness – of a place closed up for some time. The summer rains and cool season had just passed, when temperatures dropped to around 50 degrees, and skies were grey. As Europe and America were approaching autumn, and bracing for the cold northern winter, Kenya was just beginning her warmer, drier season.

During the deep sleep of that first night in our new home in the Mews of Langata, Kenya, having missed two nights of sleep while traveling, I was suddenly awoken from my slumber by a screeching sound. Sitting bolt-upright in bed, heart pounding, I tried to catch my astonished breath. Outside our doors, it seemed like prehistoric dinosaurs screamed and fought each other. My hair stood on end! What was happening? Were we being attacked by ravenous predators? Hugh laughed and told me he had experienced these same terrifying noises his first night alone there. When he enquired about them the next day, he discovered that these ear-splitting noises came from a small and harmless creature called a tree hyrax. They are about the size of a big hamster and are peaceful vegetarians. Our introduction to the incredible world of African nature had begun. It was ever full of surprising, amazing,

Rachel and Zachary with tree hyraxes (years later) when we lived at Twiga Hill Road.

wonderful and often dangerous things – often when you least expected them.

Through our brief four months in the Mews, when I would awake to a child in need of comfort in the night, and would walk down the small corridor connecting rooms, tails would slither off and disappear in front of me. There were many small openings in the structure through which outdoor creatures could come and go. I decided it was better to remain in ignorance, and not to wonder too much what creatures those tails belonged to – or to pursue them.

We both had a strong love for animals, wildlife, adventure, and less tame and less ordinary places and people. This attitude was almost a pre-requisite to living in Kenya. It stood us in good stead as many aspects of life around us began to unfold. Even the most ordinary things could be fascinating. Each day that passed gave me something new to learn or experience. There seemed to be no end to what Kenya had to share with us.

One day, as I was sweeping the living room floor, made from hard, dried mud, a leaf suddenly stood on legs and walked away. Taking a closer look, I marveled at the amazing camouflage and adaptation of this insect that looked just like a leaf. Another day, as I sat writing a letter to my parents, I looked down to see a beautiful tiny, white tree frog hanging on the side of the chair I was sitting on. And on yet another day, as I hung out the laundry on a line in front of the house, a thin, brilliant green-colored snake shot along the clothesline over my hands before I noticed it coming. I presumed it was a grass snake, but later learned that the deadly boomslang also fit that same description. The ceiling of our house was made of *makuti*, woven dried palm leaves. At night, creatures would rustle in those grasses overhead. Once, a rat fell out of it on top of us as we lay in bed asleep. No matter what, we were here now and could not afford to pay our way back. We had nothing else to go to and being here was so much more interesting than anything else we had known before.

We soon met our neighbors, whose homes were attached to ours. On our right were two nurses of British origin, Robbie and Rosemary, who worked with the Flying Doctors of Kenya. Because of the vast areas of unsettled land, making distances great, the Flying Doctors would fly to those in need out in the remote bush, as well as regularly administering all types of specialized treatments, medical care and surgery – a desperately needed service to mankind in the remote 'bush' of Kenya. Due to the enormous distances, flying is an invaluable and popular means of transportation. Private airstrips are common on farms and ranches – a necessary lifeline to their

An amazing insect camouflaged to look like a dried leaf.

existence. Robbie and Rosemary were full of interesting stories and possessed a vast knowledge of the people of Kenya. They had worked all around the country on various projects for the past 20 years.

Our neighbor to the left was a teacher at the Nairobi Academy who had also come from England. Further up, another female teacher was in the process of leaving the country. My next door neighbor introduced me to her. Dr. Joseph Popp, an American scientist and wildlife researcher, who was a friend of hers, had stopped in to say good-bye. With very few Americans living in Kenya, this introduction was to be a very significant one. Joe soon became a good friend and a frequent visitor to our home when he was in the Nairobi area. We often stayed with him in the Maasai Mara game park too.

The last dwelling in the Mews was occupied by the Norton-Griffith family. Dr. Norton-Griffith owned a business that conducted wildlife surveys, took satellite images of the changing vegetation on the plains of Kenya, and monitored other environmental factors like desertification. Their work was so ahead of their time (referring to climate change).

I would later meet Jeni and Tony Thompson, who had lived in Kenya for many years, and their young daughter Tamara. They lived just outside of the Mews, but only walking distance away. Arriving with little Zachary with his broken arm in a plaster cast, was cause for an immediate introduction via the neighbors. Zak and Tamara were close in age and it was a comfort to me that other foreign children also lived here.

Norfolk Hotel Birds by Zachary Rigby

A few months after we arrived in Kenya, Joe Popp took us into Nairobi to see the birds at the Norfolk Hotel. They had a large aviary with a variety of pretty birds in it. Joe knew the names of each kind of bird and told us all about them. One little bird would not leave our side. It was a mouse bird that loved to have its head scratched. Each time you stopped scratching, the mousebird nudged you to continue. My sister and I petted it for a long time and wished we could take it home with us.

Our 'stable' home was soon filled with lots of very interesting people. Over dinner and drinks we had vivid conversations about paleontology, anthropology and wildlife. We spent weekends visiting paleontology sites, African villages with intensely athletic dancers covered in colobus monkey skins, or observing wild animals in the Nairobi National Park.

On Friday and Saturday nights the drums would beat late into the night as the African village behind the Mews joyously celebrated the weekend. We lived only a short distance from each other, but the vegetation hid everyone from sight of each other, ensuring privacy.

I often heard baboons calling and fighting with each other behind the houses, in the vicinity of the small water tower located behind the Mews. Within days of our arrival, despite our efforts to sieve and boil the water for more than half an hour, we began having stomach pains. The water that came into our new home was rust colored, with leaves and sometimes a worm or two in it. We very quickly found out we were all suffering from life-draining amoeba, shigella and giardia dysenteries. People rarely discussed it, but they told me who to go to for treatment. Everyone just accepted this as being endemic and in true British character, grinned and put up with it, just getting on with things. Later I learned it was most likely the presence of parasites from baboon feces in our drinking water that led to us to suffering these maladies. There were no water purifying kits for sale then. Each one of us suffered from it, but Rachel and I experienced repeated bouts of it through other years we lived in Langata, sometimes being hospitalized for a week or longer. Dysentery is a huge killer in Africa. In fact, even in America, in the time of the Civil War, more people died of dysentery than from bullets.

It became clear early on that we needed to hire home help like all the other expatriates living in Nairobi. We needed an Ayah – a woman to help with cleaning the house and babysitting the children at night if we went out. All household tasks were done manually – like boiling the water, sweeping the floors with a rough broom made of small twigs, washing all the clothes by hand, making our clothes from scratch, carrying the carpets outside to clean them by beating them with a broom or stick, carrying heavy jerry cans of clean water from Nairobi, cutting the lawn using only a hand sickle or scythe. It was all back breaking, heavy work. On the flip side, many Kenyans relied on the foreigners to provide them with work and were happy to have the income. Recommendations for good workers came from our neighbors' employees, who usually had relatives looking for work.

Despite many great difficulties, this was the period of our greatest love affair with Kenya. We met so many interesting people so quickly and easily. Our social circle grew daily. Everyone was doing very interesting things and they graciously included us in activities and endeavors we might never have been a part of otherwise. The weather was gorgeous at 85 degrees and dry every day, as Nairobi was 5000 feet high and almost on the equator. The kids loved their new school, new friends, and having their Dad as their teacher, though little Zak at four years old, found the eight-to-five day very long and tiring. Academic subjects and drama lessons were followed by an hour of games in the waning afternoon sun.

The Banda was a successful academic British school. Children from the Banda School did well in life. Our kids made friends with children of diplomats, ambassadors, high ranking Kenyan politicians, and expatriates from around the world, all sharing our desire to achieve and to be successful. Hugh was very happy teaching there, as he was back in his familiar element. Instead of teaching teen-agers without parental involvement in the rough inner-city schools of my home town of Rochester, New York, he was once more teaching in the British private school system, in keeping with his own background, where parents were involved with and cared about their children's educations. Politeness and good manners were a must, and teachers were treated with respect and support. Parents were involved with school endeavors and extra activities. And, there was a high teacher to student ratio.

Within four months of moving to Kenya, we moved out of the Mews to a house on the Banda school grounds (Kisembe Estate). Hugh and our children could walk to their school classrooms each morning and night. As it was a much larger dwelling, the growing children did not have to share a bedroom like they did at the Mews. We were directly across from the Nairobi Game Park on Magadi

Road. Only a small fence and a two-lane road separated us from the lions, leopards, and other animals of the park. The clever warthogs got to know our dinner time and often appeared for 'dinner' at 6 pm, which we adored. As the animals did not know they were not supposed to cross the road, they would often wander over.

For years we listened to lions roaring at night - sometimes around the house, and sometimes out in the game park. A lion's roar alerts your every sense. A single lion close by the house, with its deep, guttural grunt, sounded so loud your every hair would stand on end. It stirred a primordial fear and created images of ancestors cringing in caves to hide from the beast, but it also made me feel safe from human attackers. I never feared 'my lions.' I just loved, respected, and admired them. Our house was set on approximately three acres and was quite isolated – especially after school had closed for the night.

Our 'dining room' table was a large wooden spool that had originally been used to transport electrical wire, which was wrapped around the spool. Our living room and bedside tables were empty wooden shipping boxes. We used and reused everything in Kenya. Nothing went to waste. The few furniture stores were very expensive. It amused us that often as electric wires or fences were put up, they would be cut down and missing in the morning. The local *wananchi* (Swahili for citizens of the country) used it for making their jewelry. They did not have electricity in their homes, so they didn't feel the loss to the country's electrical infrastructure. We had no telephone, and often no running water. Despite those drawbacks, we had many unforgettable adventures in that house. I loved its wildness, and it was always filled with fun and interesting, amazing people. The nearby Banda school swimming pool and showers, that we could walk to, made up for the fact that we often had no running water at our home.

A short distance down the road was the African village of Ongata Rongai. Down Magadi Road still further, about 70 kilometers from Nairobi, was the incredible prehistoric settlement site of early man known as Olorgesaillie – which contained the largest amount of stone tools in the world from the Acheulean or 'Hand-axe' culture, dating back 100,000 to 200,000 years. The site had been discovered by Dr. and Mrs. Louis Leakey. In those days the site

A Maasai elder near Amboseli with an oil can in his ear lobe for decoration.

had no interpretive signs and wasn't even advertised in the tourist books. There was no Visitors Center. You could pick up and touch all the objects – and take them away if you desired. There was no protection for these incredible objects of man's prehistory. The site's richness held a long time interest for me – contributing to me becoming an anthropologist and archaeologist many years later. Our friend, Dr. Joe Popp, made us aware of the site and showed and explained many of the artifacts to us. How could I not fall in love with this science of the past? It was seductive, beguiling, and so interesting!

Chapter Five
African Heritage, Night Guards, and a Crocodile

Another cool job I had was helping to manage the incredible store known as African Heritage in downtown Nairobi. They imported the most amazing pieces of art from all over Africa. One aspect of the job I loved was being a buyer of Kenyan art for the store. I met with local Kenyan artists on Thursday mornings. They would be lined up down the street by 8 am. For many, it took days to walk into Nairobi. It was hard to pass anyone by without buying something from them, knowing what they had gone through to be there.

Over time, I noticed that I had a consistent liking for the work of one young man named 'James'. His work was not of a quality suitable for the store, as it was more in the vein of folk art. But I was very fond of it, so I purchased a lot of it for myself. It managed to capture the essence of the tribal figures and animals he intended to portray.

Zak herding goats at James's mothers house.

Sharing Meat with a Lioness
by Rachel and Zachary Rigby

Our Dad must have thought he was a Kenya Cowboy. He most certainly must have been influenced by our crazy Kenya Cowboy friends who had no fear of wild animals. We were in the Nairobi National Park, driving around, when we came upon a lioness on a zebra she had killed and was eating. A close distance from the carcass was the zebra's tail. It had been severed and was lying next to the zebra's body. Without saying a word, Dad jumped out of the car and grabbed it! We were shocked. Lucky for us all, the lioness let him have it. We felt lucky to still have a Father. We hung up the tail in our shed after putting salt on it, hoping to dry it out and keep it for a memento, but it quickly became full of maggots. It stunk badly!

Lioness on a zebra kill.

James was a Maasai who lived a three-day walk outside of Nairobi. He once invited us to visit his manyatta, where he lived with his mother, sister and family. We made the long drive out to their home made of dried cow dung and mud, sitting on the wide open expanse of dry plains. It had a yard surrounded by thick thorn bush fence to help protect those inside from lion attacks. James' family were very gracious, especially towards our young son, but we did not know how to speak Maa and they did not speak English.

The boys of the family showed Zak how they herded goats and invited him to accompany them, giving him some good walking sticks to play the role. We adults sat in the shade outside. Like all married Maasai women, the women's heads were clean shaven, and they were covered in beaded ornamentation. The young men grew long, plaited braids that they covered in the red ochre earth of Kenya. They also wore beaded ornaments and some jewelry.

Violent attacks in Kenya were becoming commonplace. Twenty-man gangs would sometimes raid houses at night. My friend Heather's father, John Alexander, was brutally hacked to pieces in his home on Kisembe Estate, only three houses down the road from us. Robbery was a possible motive, but we all felt we were sitting targets. So, we hired a security guard, known as an *Askari*. Our *askari*, Iboningi, came from the Samburu tribe, a Maa speaking people from northern Kenya. They are a Nilotic people who live as semi-nomadic pastoralists, herding cattle, sheep, goats and camels.

The Samburu diet consists mainly of a drink made by mixing a cow's blood with milk. They put the drink in gourds that have been cleaned using cow urine, so there is a taste of that in the drink as well. They collect the blood by shooting an arrow into the jugular vein of the cow, and draining the blood into a cup. The wound is then quickly sealed with hot ash. Meat is only consumed on special occasions. The Samburu diet is supplemented with roots, vegetables and tubers dug up and made into a soup. Both men and women wear colorful beaded earrings, necklaces and bracelets. Samburu men also paint their faces, using striking patterns to accentuate their facial features, often making them look more ferocious.

Adult Samburu men sometimes went to the cities to work as guards. They were highly sought after because of their strong reputation as warriors. Iboningi was known to someone who worked at the Banda School, and they introduced him to us.

The township of Ongata Rongai was not far down the road from our house. It was a settlement outside of Nairobi, favored by Nairobi's huge workforce. Many muggers and armed-robbers lived there and laid in wait for both innocent pedestrians and motorists. (Info from *The Nairobian*)

In the night, these bandits would walk to our house, braving the roaming lions and leopards, to attack our house, which was closest to the road. We felt exposed, vulnerable and alone on three acres of land with several acres of school land surrounding it on one side, and the Nairobi National Park on the other.

Dressed only in a simple *shuka*, a striking red cotton cloth wrapped around his waist, with a woolen blanket over the top for warmth, Iboningi stood guard throughout the night, often singing. He used arrows and a bow as his weapons of defense. Like most Kenyans, Somalis and people from the Yemen, he chewed the plant known as *Miraa* or *Khat*. The leaf and stem are used as a recreational drug and as medicine. It is used very often as a stimulant, similar to amphetamines, to increase alertness, to make one hyperactive, more aggressive, and to bring on insomnia.

Kath "buying" miraa or khat.

Our German Shepherd, 'Jaws,' and our mixed breed dog called 'Hyena' kept Iboningi company during his long nightly vigils. I would awaken many times during the night and listen for Iboningi's singing, but when 'my' lions in the game park just across the road were roaring, I felt the safest of all, as if they were our personal watchdogs.

Our house had an enclosed glass veranda where we could watch animals walk by under the Ngong Hills, while eating our meals. Off the veranda, leading deeper into the house, security became more intense, with a metal door and metal brackets that held three 2 x 4 wooden planks, which we would put into the brackets as reinforcement against break-ins. All the windows had metal bars on them. *Pangas (machetes)*, spears and *rungus* (a wooden club with a bulbous head) were in the corners of the rooms, ready for sudden use. Finally, we had a ladder going up to the roof as the last retreat. We had more weapons stashed there for defense.

I hated to live under this kind of fear, and I always felt that Kenyan people were basically good people. Some felt they had to steal just to live. The Kenya government then had very little in place to care for the welfare of Kenya's people's. On the edges of Nairobi, many lived in cardboard shacks, without sewage or running water. Social Security to them was having as many children as you possibly could, in the hopes that one may take care of you later in old age.

In 1983 my spine and neck were broken when I was a passenger on a motorcycle. I was sent back to the U.S. for medical treatment. During this time I stayed at my parents' home. One afternoon they were out and I was there by myself. The doorbell rang. I instantly hit the floor trying to hide! There was no guard outside and I was panic-stricken. I looked around for a weapon but could find none. I stayed low so that no one could see me inside the house. In time, I crept up to the window and looked over the ledge, just in time to see my uncle walking away. It was then that I realized how much the frequent attacks by gangs in Kenya had affected me. Life in Kenya seemed to be getting more and more dangerous.

One day Iboningi asked if he could have some time off to go back to his home. We enquired if everything was all right. He replied, "*Bwana*, someone has stolen my shoes. I must go back."

When he returned, we asked if things at his home were satisfactory. "Yes, *Bwana*, he is dead," was all he said.

One weekend a group of Banda School teachers and parents decided to take their children on a camping trip away from Nairobi and the school. They camped many hours' drive out of town. During the day, the temperature got very hot and the children begged to go swimming in the nearby lake. The adults decided to let them cool off, making them stay near the shore. The water was colored dark by the tannins from the trees, making it a muddy brown color. You could not see what lay below the surface.

A short time after the children entered the water, a child screamed and violent thrashing began. A crocodile had a child in its mouth! Sean Jackson, Deputy Head Master of the Banda School at the time, jumped into the water, poking the crocodile in the eyes to try to make it release the child. Other parents jumped in to help, too. To everyone's great relief, miraculously, the crocodile released the child and he was carried to safety. But health care and a hospital were still a long distance away. The child had suffered

Halloween by Rachel Rigby

Halloween was a very special time for those of us living in Kenya with American mothers. We had parties with costumes and images of ghosts. Mom hung skeletons and scary decorations around the place. The Kenyans didn't join in the laughter or take any of this lightly. They were very concerned and thought that we were doing witchcraft. They were noticeably nervous and on guard. Sometimes, they would not show up for work when we had the parties. They visibly relaxed when the decorations came down. Witchcraft was a very real and very negative thing in their lives – not make-believe like it was for us *wazungu*. They also felt that chameleons had a special spiritual power and were very afraid of them.

Halloween Party

numerous puncture wounds and the putrid teeth of a crocodile are covered in strong bacteria.

He would almost certainly have bled to death during the long drive back to Nairobi, except for one lucky thing. There was a baby with the group and the parents had brought lots of cloth diapers. These were put to good use, binding the streaming bite wounds and stemming the flow of blood. The lucky child survived the terrifying ordeal. Without Sean's extremely quick, brave action the story would have ended tragically. Note to self, "Our children will never cool off in the water, no matter how hot it gets."

It is truly miraculous that Sean managed to get the crocodile to give up the boy. Nile crocodiles can grow up to 20 feet long and weigh a ton. One swipe from the powerful tail would have broken

Kissing *Twigas* by Zak Rigby

Twigas are giraffes in Swahili. Mom found out about the Nairobi Giraffe Center, when she went to interview for a job with the Leslie-Melvilles. It was located close to our house. There was a high platform that we could climb up to feed the giraffes from our hands. It was as high as their heads. My sister would put the food in her mouth and the giraffes would 'kiss' her to get it. Yuk is all I can say! Those poor giraffes. Girl cooties! They were a special kind of giraffe called Rothschild's that only live in Kenya and Uganda. Humphrey, a Kenyan man who works there, says they are very rare. The center is new and I love going there. We took our Grandad when he came to visit us. He loved it too.

Rachel giving food to a giraffe with her mouth.

Sean's bones and knocked him off his feet or unconscious. It is also amazing that other crocodiles didn't join in the attack – especially with other people in the water. Crocodiles have a bite force of 3,700 pounds per square inch (psi) – almost four times more than a hyena, lion or tiger! A human bite force is only 150 to 200 psi.

Crocodiles can stay invisible to the sharpest of eyes. Their nostrils, ears and eyes are located on top of their heads, which enables them to see, hear and smell their prey, while their huge body stays hidden under the water. Once it spots its prey, crocodiles dive down without leaving a ripple, and submerge completely by exhaling some air from its lungs as it moves closer to the prey. Special pressure sensing pits enable the crocodile to navigate in the muddy water. When the prey is in striking range, the beast unleashes a deadly jump using its legs – which can be as fast as 40 feet per second. It then uses its strong tail as a propeller to gain more momentum, emerging out of the water to grab the prey. Once caught, the crocodile drags the prey to deeper waters and uses its strength to drown its victim.

Chapter Six
My First Real Job in Kenya

Shortly after arriving, I began a very interesting job in the development field with a London-based company known as Intermediate Technology Development Group (ITDG). I was introduced to the Africa Director through friends we had made when we lived in Manchester, England. My boss was Mr. Richard Whitcombe, a Canadian who covered large parts of Africa for ITDG. I ran the company in Kenya in his absence. The company assisted Kenyan people, often living in remote areas, with affordable technological improvements to tools they used every day. The company's principals were firmly based on preserving natural resources. I used the anthropological techniques of participant observation and open-ended interviews decades before I ever got a Master's Degree in the field of Anthropology. I visited different groups of people and discussed and observed their natural resource uses with them, such as the amount of firewood they needed. I then discussed my findings with appropriate technology engineers, connecting both parties. Together we came up with a design for an improved *jiko*, an inexpensive portable cooking oven that was so heavily insulated it used far less firewood, thereby saving natural resources. It was very satisfying as it combined two of my biggest desires - to help the environment and to help people. I also arranged further education in England and America for Kenyan officials who had been identified as future leaders of the country.

The office was located in downtown Nairobi. After several years of happy work, the Norfolk Hotel (only one block away from the office) was blown up on New Year's Eve, while packed with many unsuspecting, innocent people. This bombing was carried out by a middle eastern terrorist, in retaliation for the Israeli raid on Entebbe to free Jewish hostages held in a plane hijacking. The bombing targeted the Norfolk Hotel because it belonged to the Block family, who were Jewish. Living across from the Game Park in Langata, we heard the explosion from 11 miles away. I drove in to try and find out the state of my office building the next day. Despite climbing over strewn debris, I was unable to gain access to the company office, which remained blocked for a number of weeks. ITDG decided to leave Kenya and that happy job came to an end. I never saw Richard again.

However, in the course of the meetings that Richard and I attended with numerous UN agencies and other non-governmental non-profit organizations, I soon met people who would change the lives of the members of my family forever. One such talented, friendly, and fun person was George McBean, a Scotsman who was very creative, a good musician and photographer. I asked him to join my band, which had become very successful, but he travelled around Africa for UNICEF too often to join us. George was already solidly gray at the ripe old age of twenty-something, when we met him. He said it worked to his advantage as he was given far more respect than he ever deserved because of his gray hair. Several years later, when George was transferred to another country by UNICEF, Hugh took over his job.

Another key person I met was Phil Hasrick, a young American who worked for UNICEF. Phil could not get over how I arrived in Kenya and very soon after had a job with the respected NGO - ITDG. Work permits for expatriate women were very difficult to obtain. In the course of one of our discussions, I told Phil that Hugh's terms at the school could not support our family, and asked if there was anything that Hugh could do for UNICEF. Phil very kindly asked about Hugh's skills and checked around. He found that they could use someone who could do graphics work that could teach health lessons through art. Kenya had many different tribal groups who spoke different dialects and languages. So art could demonstrate a message that language could not. Hugh did a trial poster for Phil which started five years of freelance work for Hugh with UNICEF. Eventually the work became full time, but because of a quota system, they were not allowed to hire a person of British descent, a category that was over-represented. So, we lived on month-to-month contracts with UNICEF for a number of years. We now had to pay for each semester of the very expensive private schools that both our children attended. Tuition for this primary school cost about the same as a semester of a state college in the US. Our landlady also required a year's lease from us, which had no provision for losing one's employment. We held our breath, hoped for the best, and kept putting one foot in front of the other.

Chapter Seven
Baboons and Safaris

Every day, every outing was exciting. The world was full of new things and new sights to marvel over, like beautifully woven African houses made of rushes or palms. We visited markets full of new African items, unusual fruits and vegetables, and artwork we'd never seen before. Plants like papaya, passion fruit, bananas and avocados grew in our back yard. We went on safari every chance we could. Every weekend we stayed in Nairobi, we went to the Nairobi Game Park. The gate was directly across the street from the Banda School.

We visited and camped at Amboseli National Park, where elephants sometimes leaned against our tent in the night. We often went on safaris to Mombasa, too, taking the overnight train from our 5,000 feet high elevation to the ocean, where we snorkeled on the gorgeous reefs. Once, Hugh and I climbed the dormant volcano, Mt. Longonot. We took lots of other safaris with Dr. Martin Pickford, Paleontologist for the Nairobi National Museum and his wife, Jill, and their family. Sometimes we went far up country where it was very remote and unpopulated, on museum paleontology explorations and assignments with Martin. Being taken behind the scenes at the museum, seeing the artifacts and early hominid discoveries that Martin and other scientists had made, in addition to these trips, was so exciting, it led me to work for museums later in my life.

But the most incredible thing for us to do was to visit Dr. Joe Popp, head of the Harvard Baboon Research Project in the Maasai Mara. Sometimes we went as a family. The children had their birthdays there. Sometimes we brought other teachers from the Banda. And sometimes I would be flown down in a tiny airplane to work with the research team. Large numbers of zebra ran across the airstrip right up until the very last minute, looking beautiful and amazing, but making for some tense landings and take offs. Birds would fly in front of the tiny bush planes too.

Rachel and Zachary with two of the Pickford girls and Martin Pickford on the Nairobi National Museum Land Rover.

Baboon research was dangerous work. We would put down lines of corn kernels, then wait for the alpha males to get into a bitter fight. When one got injured, we would dart it with a tranquilizer and separate it from the rest of the troop, putting a sack over its head to disorient it if it woke up, and to lessen its deadly bite. Then we would carry it into the back of the open-sided Jeep - next to me! If it woke up, BOOM – I WAS IT! Their canine teeth can be two inches - longer than a lion's! And their disposition could be fiercely aggressive. Next, we measured and recorded its wounds, took dental molds and blood work and gave it a thorough physical exam. We then put it in a metal cage to protect it from other animals until it had regained consciousness, at which time we returned him back near his troop. We always had to be watching all around during these proceedings. We worked on the ground of the game park, which was absolutely loaded with all kinds of wild animals. We looked small and defenseless huddled over the baboon while we worked on the ground. This was a predator's dream.

A leopard's favorite food is baboon. Once, Joe barely managed to escape from an attacking leopard while performing these tests on an anesthetized baboon. I was not there that day, but if his assistant had not seen the leopard running full pelt at him and warned him in the nick of time, he would not have known to run to the safety of the vehicle. He barely made it! Lions and cape buffalo, leopards, wild dogs, other males of the baboon troop, rhinos, elephants and hyenas could all come around at any time while we were working on the ground in the game park.

Sometimes, we visited Rosemary, a young Maasai woman who spoke English. The government had required each Maasai family to select at least one daughter to go to school. Rosemary had been chosen. In Rosemary's home, made of dried cattle dung and sticks, she took us inside where they kept young cows and goats for protection from lions, and explained how everything was done, how their society was organized, social norms, how things functioned, etc. She was a fascinating source of knowledge regarding the Maasai people. The darkness inside the house and the smell of the urine and feces of the animals, together with the smoke from the fire, made it difficult to breathe.

Dr. Joe Popp, his research assistant, Kathy and kids by Joe's jeep at the Mara River. The Maasai wander the game park freely and always seem to show up when you stop.

Hugh and Kath with teacher friends from the Banda School and Rosemary - outside of her manyatta.

Joe introduced us to Laurence Frank who was a PhD student studying hyenas at the time. Laurence and Joe both worked at the Mara Research Station, although they studied different animals for different projects. Laurence was very enthusiastic about his research. We were thrilled when he very kindly took us out on night drives and gave us night goggles to observe the hyenas. I was amazed how well they worked. It was fascinating to learn that hyenas are often thought to be hermaphrodites because females are born with genitalia that resembles male sex organs. Laurence is now Dr. Laurence Frank and has been researching lions for a number of years. He is a Research Associate with UC Berkeley.

When I later learned that Laurence was working with lions, I thought what extraordinary courage that must take. Hyenas were very fearsome, but the might of lions always commands the greatest respect. I remember thinking that Laurence was fearless and how I would be too frightened to be able to do that. I hoped he would somehow remain unscathed. Baboons were scary enough for me to work with!

Wildlife researchers face more subtle dangers too. I remember Laurence talking about a dead Thomson's gazelle that he had found without signs of trauma, with just a little blood around its nose. Due to his lack of experience in those days, Laurence assumed it had been killed by a cheetah that had been scared off, so he brought it home and was butchering it in front of the dwelling where he and his wife and newborn daughter lived at the research station, with the idea of having it for dinner.

By the most unbelievable coincidence (or was it fate?) a young man walked by and wanted to take a look. The man was a Canadian veterinarian who was with a visiting research group. He recognized the symptoms of anthrax. After learning this, Laurence and his family were terrified they would get it and drew blood from each other to send to Nairobi for testing. His highly experienced veterinarian friend, Lars Karstad, specialized in wildlife diseases. "Lars was more interested in the fact that they had found anthrax, as it had not been recorded in Kenya in decades, than he was concerned about the likelihood of us catching it," said a joking Laurence. Needless to say, it was an interesting few days for them, as they all expected to die. "My wife made me boil everything in the house - including the rug. Since then I have been up to my elbows in rabid hyenas and jackals, but I treat suspicious wildlife deaths with a great deal more respect than I did as a callow youth," he says.

Joe had a permit for his research team to take walking safaris on the Serengeti Plains of the Maasai Mara. During these safaris, we walked into lions hiding along the sides of game trails, lions on a kill, lions mating, herds of Cape buffalo and much more. We only had one rifle to protect ourselves. Fortunately, we never had to use it. On one of our walking research days, we were about to cross a small stream. Bushes lined the trail. Suddenly, we heard a lioness's low growl. She came out towards us from under the cover. We had to stand still and face her without moving. The sun beat down, sweat started dripping into our eyes. Flies dive bombed into our eyes and made us want to chase them away, but we couldn't. Joe had his rifle ready and trained on her. It seemed like forever before we could slowly back away from her. She finally went back to hide under her bush, waiting for an unsuspecting animal to cross.

When we got far enough away, we decided it was time for a drink and snack break and we sat down. In a short while, I felt sharp bites on my legs. Soon I felt more and more. I absolutely had to do something about it. I ran, casting my clothes off as I went - down to my underwear. I had sat down in a line of Army ants,

Dr Joe Popp and members of his research team walking through the Maasai Mara.

called *siafu*! They are like land piranhas and if left untouched, can strip a body to the bone. I totally lost my dignity, but I saved my life. No more sitting!

Unfortunately, Joe's project came to an end several years after we moved to Kenya. We were all blessed to learn so much about the animals from Joe, to be able to stay at the Research Station whenever we wanted, and to go around the game park with Joe. I was able to take part in the work. He was brilliant and funny and always had a new scientific hypothesis he wanted to test, some of them ahead of their time. He scientifically set about getting as large and fat as he could – just to test how it happened. When he felt he had gotten as large as he could, he then set about getting as thin as he could. He became a runner and ran marathons with the

Charging Rhinos by Zachary Rigby

We often spend days observing the wildlife in Nairobi Game Park across the street from our wild Langata home. When we first went to Nairobi in 1979, it was not uncommon to see 22 rhinos in an afternoon, my parents tell me. On this day, we had stopped close to a rhino and her baby when our ancient Volkswagen beetle, over 20 years of age, cut out. A rhino's eyesight is very poor, so she did not see us and was not alarmed. But when she got our scent on the wind, it was a different story. She immediately went into attack mode thinking she needed to protect her baby. She came charging, barreling along! I was on the side of the tiny car nearest to her. Dad kept trying to start the car and the rhino kept getting closer. I got more and more frightened, nearly crawling on top of my sister to get as far away as I could from the charging horn. Finally, the car battery turned over and we started to move away, but the rhino was gaining ground. The rhino slammed into the side of the car, but since my Dad was now "gassing it, pedal to the metal," to get out of harm's way, the damage was not catastrophic. I was terrified out of my nine-year-old mind, but I survived! I never forgot the experience.

incredible Kenyan runners. Joe undoubtedly was part of the reason I became an anthropologist in later years. Through him and his brilliant mind, I grew to love science and academia. He was always teaching about something, and I was all ears, soaking up as much as I could learn.

We took many safaris with Julia Glen and her children. We would set up our camp tables under yellow thorn trees for the umbrella like canopy of shade that they offered, which was better than none. One time we wound up in territory that had herds of African cattle with a fatty hump on their backs. They were resistant to harsh conditions and could survive on poor grazing and rocky terrain. That night we were all covered in hundreds of ticks and had to spray our skin with OFF from head to toe. Amazingly, no one got a tick borne disease. We visited Julia's brother Nigel at his farm on the slopes of Mt. Kenya, where he raised sheep and grew grain for market. The children fed the sheep with baby bottles and got rides on Nigel's *piki-piki* (dirt bike motorcycle).

One safari when Rob joined us was particularly crazy. As we set up our tent, I looked out at the shore of Lake Baringo. I saw our children with the Glen children out in the lake in flimsy reed boats made by the Njemps people using a local reed call *ambatch*. I thought they looked like they were made of banana leaves. The children had found the boats on the shoreline. No one had seen them go out. As they got further out, the children got nervous and were starting to get into the water to try to swim back to shore.

Our kids on Lake Baringo with the Njemps woven boats they found.

But they were too far out for six- and eight-year-olds to swim back, not to mention the crocodiles and hippos that were between them and the shoreline. We shouted and convinced them to stay in the boats and paddle for shore. There was no other boat to get out to rescue them, and to have swum out into the water with the crocs and hippos would have been equally disastrous. Luckily, the kids somehow paddled back safely. They were a little shaken up, but fine. I, on the other hand, had aged ten years!

Chapter Eight
Spiders That Ate Mice and Birds

Our house on Kisembe Estate was located on the Athi Plains. Those plains teemed with life – not always life you would like to see. One of the sights we would have chosen not to encounter was an African tarantula, known to us as the Baboon spider. Like many things, they were in our house in numbers. Since they were usually not in plain view, when you came upon them, it was quite startling. To see a spider so large, so thick and heavy bodied, so hairy and menacing-looking when you least expected to see anything, could cause quite a fright. Especially the first time – when we didn't even know such a creature existed! They have long fangs, and possess venom glands, producing a painful bite. With a leg span of six inches, they were the size of dinner plates! We learned that they ate small vertebrates like geckos, beetles, grasshoppers and crickets, millipedes, and even scorpions, mice and birds!

At one point, we started seeing so many of them that I became concerned for the children. So, we managed to capture one that was lying in wait behind a picture on the wall. It was difficult to find a jar large enough to squeeze it into. I drove it into the Nairobi National Museum to ask someone there about it. The entomologist there said if the children were bitten, we should get them to the hospital for anti-biotics or they could get septicemia. With anti-biotics, they should survive. I felt somewhat better knowing these spiders didn't have a venom that could kill quickly like so many of our snakes did. By now we knew they lived behind every picture or hanging basket in the house.

Still, you can imagine my surprise when one night I went to bed late and pulled back the blankets. In my sleepy haze, I realized there was a large baboon spider in my bed! It reared up on its long, hairy back legs with its front legs raised to fight me. It was then that I saw its downward facing red fangs! I dispatched it with a club that I kept by the side of the bed in case of attack (by humans).

I reminded myself that we had moved to Kenya because of our love of the natural world and the beautiful animals in it. I can't say I ever grew to love any spiders, or to find them beautiful, but it was the perfect example of respecting the creatures we learned about and observed - that we had never known existed. We were interested and fascinated by all of these amazing creatures we discovered on a regular basis. Each one had a purpose and a role to play in our interlocked creation on earth, but please, just not in our beds! Even to this day, we always shake out our shoes before we put them on. This was a habit we started when living in Kenya.

Poisonous snakes were a regular occurrence at our home on the *vlei* (Athi Plains.) One Saturday two teachers from the Banda visited us. Our dog, Jaws, was tied to the tree a short distance from the front door. Our young son, Zachary, was playing at our feet. The front door was open, as it normally was. Jaws began barking. We paid no attention, thinking he just wanted to get off the chain and go visit the people who were attending an event across the field at the Banda school. In time, our friends got ready to leave. As we walked towards the front door, little Zak (then four years old) who was barefoot, led the way. He was just about to step off the front step when Hugh spotted the large puff adder hidden at the base of the step. Hugh swiftly put his hands under Zak's armpits and lifted him out of danger in the very nick of time. Jaws had been trying to warn us all along.

Hugh with our children holding a python (a constrictor, not poisonous)

Getting Bitten by Zak Rigby

One day I was playing with my friend Marcus, who lived down our street. We went into a neighbor's yard and I climbed over a fence I shouldn't have. They had a kali (fierce) dog that bit me. Luckily, its owner came out and got me out of there. The dog could have had rabies, but I never told my mother. She would have been upset and told me I shouldn't have been doing what I did. She would have taken me to the doctors to get anti-rabies shots. I didn't want that! Glad I didn't get rabies.

Lions Visit the Banda School –
"Sir, There are Lions Outside of our Classroom Windows"

The Banda School was located on the Athi Plains in Langata, directly across the street from the Nairobi Game Park, which was a short distance outside of Nairobi. As Nairobi suburbs went, it bordered the suburb of Karen, where the famous Isak Dinesen (Karen Blixen) of Out of Africa fame had lived on her farm. The Nairobi Game Park had broken, tumbled down fences to keep animals in. There was only a two lane road between the school and the Game Park which had no traffic at night. These (almost) suburbs were not like suburbs in developed countries.

Lions under the classroom windows distracted the students while taking their exams.

They were inhabited by wild animals and lots of them were large predators.

One year near the end of the school year, the Banda school students were taking their Common Entrance exams to get into Secondary Schools in the UK. Lions decided to pay the school a visit. As the children tried to concentrate on their exams, the lions were raising themselves up on hind legs to look in the windows and to breathe heavily while slobbering on the louvered windows. After the lions left, the students completed their exams and the children were again free to go out of doors. The Headmaster had to send a note with the exams saying the results may not have been as good as they otherwise might have been, as the children were distracted by lions under their classroom windows.

A Hard Rain Falls

The rain had been pouring down since the night before. Rains in this part of the world are rare. The soil bakes hard. It cracks, sometimes making deep caverns, it is so dry. Water is in constant short supply. Together with the high equatorial heat, droughts and famines often occur because of the lack of rain. Dying from lack of water is not unusual. The monsoon season is what sustains the great amount of life that exists in Kenya. April and May are the heaviest rainy season - the long rains. In November, there are short rains. But this rain on May 8, 1986, was exceptionally heavy and hard – even for the rainy season.

Driving home from working in Nairobi that day I witnessed some extraordinarily frightening and sad things. Nairobi is a city where many thousands of workers walk to work – often very long distances – no matter what the weather is doing. It is common to see many, many people walking on the sides of the roads. Others catch *matatus*, privately owned vans that provide public transportation to the *wananchi* (Kenyan people) for a fee.

I didn't take my usual route home on this day because there appeared to be heavy flooding on the Uhuru Highway. Instead, I turned onto smaller roads which I knew came out on the Langata Road by Wilson Airport. There were vast amounts of Kenyan workers walking on the road, trying to get home before dark in this torrential rain. A short distance ahead of me was a small bridge

The Little Creature by Zachary Rigby

We were returning from a safari in Tanzania. We had just crossed the border back into Kenya. There was no food or cold soda in Tanzania, so on the way home we stopped to get a drink at the first place we could find. It was hot and we were so thirsty. While my parents sat cooling off, I went exploring. I found a tiny, mouse-like creature with huge ears at the base of a tree! We thought it had fallen out of its nest in the tree tops. I brought it back to my parents, who put it into a match box until we could get a doll's bottle to feed it. The little creature thrived on the milk we fed it. It would run up on our shoulders and sit there and sleep. When I went to school and Mom went to work, she took it to the KSPCA down the road who babysat for it during the daytime. They consulted a veterinarian who also didn't know what it was. It may have been a new species unknown to anyone. The next time we went on safari we took it with us. It was still a baby and needed to be fed every couple of hours. Unfortunately, my sister wanted it to be free, not realizing that it needed us to keep it alive. She let it go in the Game Park. We still wonder what it was!

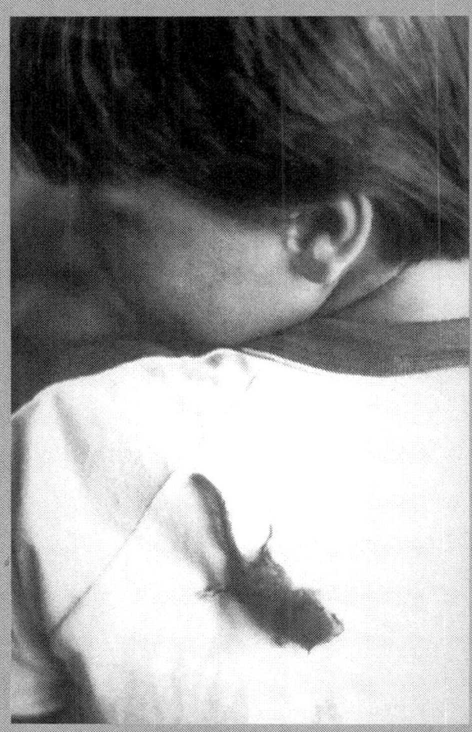

The tiny never-identified creature on Zachary's back.

with cars and people crossing over it. Suddenly, a monumental wall of flood water swept down onto the bridge from above, sweeping people and cars over the side of the ravine – like a tsunami - until the bridge itself collapsed. The force of the flash flood was tremendous. I was shocked and horrified for the poor unfortunates caught up in it. If I had been just a few moments earlier, just one more car ahead, and it would have been me too! I'll never forget seeing those poor people being helplessly carried away to their deaths, their eyes and faces a mass of shock and terror as they were swept over the edge. It was too dangerous to stay in the area, as the flood waters continued flowing, leaving me as helpless as the other people were, despite having a car. All I could do was watch in horror and sadness. I managed to turn around and had to then brave the flooding on Uhuru Highway that I had earlier tried to avoid.

I arrived home four hours later than usual, in the dark, to find Hugh and the kids safely home, and Joe Popp waiting there to see if I had made it back safely. He was a good friend and often visited when he came into town. Friends in Kenya were very close, helping each other through many things. In my melancholy misery, it was comforting to share this traumatic event with people who also cared about these poor souls and understood the pain of it. Joe had encountered difficulties getting through Nairobi to Langata from the Maasai Mara too.

My heart went out to the many people who suffered or died that day. Many lost their lives in the terrible force of those rough and powerful waters. Nature reminded us that day that we are all only guests on this planet.

Heather Alexander and I became friendly when I was a singer. Her father, who ran a safari business, lived just down the road from us on Kisembe Estate. Heather had come out to Kenya from England to live with her father for a while. During this time, two of her close friends came out to visit her from England. Heather secured the services of her father's safari company and kindly invited me to join them for a five-day safari to Samburu Game Park.

We went to remote Samburu National Park in a season when there did not appear to be any other visitors at all. It was a heavenly time, peacefully spent viewing wildlife. The setting was extremely isolated and we never saw another human being outside of our group in the five days we were there. Due to its remote distance and the fact that it was inaccessible for many years, the park has retained a serene and quiet feeling. Besides the numerous wildlife found in the game reserve, the park is also a bird haven with many beautiful hornbills. We saw herds of elephants playing in the river – a sight that always brought joy untold. The juveniles covered themselves in the water, rolling in it, filling their trunks and spraying it over their heads and bodies, sparring with each other. Adults delighted in baths, submersing themselves in full. But the babies were the funniest sight. They were so ecstatic, they ran around and contorted their little bodies into every conceivable shape, being so filled with joy and play and utter carefree abandon, that they did not know what to do with themselves. Watching elephants bathe in the river was one of the most special sights I have ever witnessed. It was a spectacle I could never tire of.

As we drove on, we witnessed the sturdy large body and splendid prehistoric beak of a Kori Bustard, Africa's heaviest flying bird, standing tall and striding across the vast grass plain in search of an evening meal. Kori Bustards range in weight from 24-42 pounds, are omnivorous, with insects making a large part of their diets as well as a variety of small mammals, lizards, snakes, seeds and berries. I marveled at the sight of this creature that looked as if it did not belong to this time period of history. We also loved the beautiful, long-legged, elegant secretary bird that was looking for a snake to eat. As well as being so dignified and beautiful, she kills and eats snakes – venomous ones included. The secretary bird is a fearsome, aggressive predator. Found on the open grasslands of sub-Saharan Africa, this four-an-a-half foot-tall bird, has quill-like feathers that emerge from its head crest. It kills its prey by striking it with its claw using incredible speed and precision.

While out on a game drive, we spotted a tiny dik dik trying to hide itself in the bushes on the side of the road. We got out to look more closely at it lying down trying to be invisible. Its delicate frame and fragile physique were stunningly beautiful. Even when they are adults, they are no larger than a white tail deer's fawn. I wanted to protect the gentle creature from the fierce predators that abounded in the wilderness of the reserve, but I had to respect and accept the laws of nature.

A Dog as a Cat's Mom by Zak Rigby

It was school holidays and Mom took me and Johnny and Ryan Eames to the KSPCA (Kenya Society for the Protection of Animals) to see the animals - for something to do to keep us amused. Before we went inside, Mom said sternly, "Promise you won't ask for any more animals. We have three dogs and the landlady has six horses at our house. It's enough." Within a minute of walking in, she saw a tiny Siamese kitten. I never saw Mom move so quickly to get something in her whole life. She was shaking, she wanted this tiny fluffball so badly. We got the kitten and left to go back home immediately with it. We kids didn't get to see any of the animals. Our visit was all over in a flash! We called the tiny kitten Posho after the cornmeal that the Kenyans ate. When it was cooked, the corn was whitish like the kittens body, and the edges were brown, like the border colors of the kitten.

When our big Doberman, Eva, saw the tiny kitten, she had a similar reaction to Mom. She was immediately in love with it and thought the kitten was her baby. She would lick it and lie down and suckle the kitten. When they went outside, Eva would walk over the top of the kitten because we had many, many hawks and some eagles too. Eva knew the danger they posed more than we did and she did this on her own. That's how smart she was. She did this until Posho was fully grown. This was the same dog that kept a male intruder pinned down for a whole afternoon. She never bit him or attacked him. She just growled at him if he moved. After several hours, the man got tired and laid down on the grass. She sat on him to make sure he didn't go anywhere. Eva was the best dog ever!

Zak and our Doberman Eva, the best dog ever!

In the evening, our African cook would make a fire on the ground and prepare a first rate hot meal out in the open. It was amazing the beautiful cuisine these cooks could produce on an open fire. They even baked fresh bread by digging a hole in the ground to make an oven, covering the pan with hot coals. Card tables were covered in white linen tablecloths and they set fine china on our table in the virgin wilderness. The cook served us wine, wearing white gloves. I have never eaten finer meals. Our family safaris never had a cook nor the finer specialty items that a professional safari company provided, so I reveled in the beautiful contrast of it all. We slept in tents beneath the stars, listening to the sounds of wildlife during the nights.

One afternoon we stood at a slight elevation on the side of the Ewaso Nyiro River, looking into the thick muddy brown water. We could see nothing below the surface. But within just a few short moments, two enormous crocodiles came out of the water

Jaws and Hyena Get in a Scrap by Rachel Rigby

One night there was a sound like a BIG rattle coming from outside the house on the front lawn. The dogs were outside, barking non-stop. When we opened the door to see what was happening, we saw that the dogs were trying to tackle a huge porcupine. Wow! We never knew how big they were. We tried to call the dogs to come in the house, but they weren't having any of it. This was too exciting for them. It was not possible for Dad and Mom to go out and pull them in as porcupine quills were flying in the air and could be very dangerous. In the morning the dogs came in with their faces full of embedded quills. Lucky for them, none of them had found their eyes, but their noses were swollen and painful looking. Some quills were embedded in their sinuses. The dogs weren't looking so excited about this encounter now. We carefully removed each quill and put disinfectant on the opening. It would have been a painful way to die from infection. Lions and other predators experience this and can die from infection. We still have some of those quills to this day. Chalk one up to the porcupine!

Being Artists by Zak & Rachel Rigby

Our Dad had a degree in Art and a Master's Degree in Education. He taught art at a Junior High School in Rochester, NY, USA, and later at the Banda School in Kenya. There were a lot of artists who sold their work in Kenya. One weekend Dad decided he was going to make some of his own artwork and he asked us if we would like to make some too. We each came away with some beautiful prints from lino cuts that we really enjoyed making. We sold our work at some art shows. We kids got to keep our own money to buy toys, ice cream, or whatever we wanted! We liked having our own money, and it was a lot of fun to show people our art work. They seemed to like it. It was a real introduction to understanding what the life of an artist might be like too.

Zak's lino print

Rachel's lino print

following the sounds of our voices. We had a slight advantage, being a little elevated and being a short distance from the water's edge, but crocodiles can run very quickly. They live between 70 to 100 years and weigh 500 to 2,200 pounds, ranging from 7 feet to 16 feet in length. It is amazing how fast they can cover ground when pursuing something. Of course, most of the time they ambush from beneath the cover of the water. Nonetheless, we wisely retreated back to the safety of the vehicle. Any injury in such a remote location would never be good.

Chapter Nine
The Band Cactus

While still new to Kenya, Hugh drove across the *vlei* (flat field) to the *Duka* (a small grocery store) so he could use the telephone booth outside of the store to make a telephone call. We did not have a telephone. It had been raining and not having lived there for long, he did not know that you should stay on paved roads when it has been raining. We had not yet learned about black cotton soil. So, Hugh proceeded to drive across the *vlei* over the unpaved red murram road, until he met black cotton soil. It is not always easy to see the difference in soils, but if it has been raining, the black cotton soil acts like quick sand and it sucks and grips the car's tires tightly. The car became mired down and firmly stuck, so he walked the rest of the way to the *duka* in the storm. Upon arriving, he stepped into the phone booth to find the bottom of it under about three inches of water. As he stood in the water, using the phone, lightning struck the booth. Amazingly, it did not kill Hugh or even do much physical damage to him. He only complained about feeling tired and "frazzled."

I also had to learn about black cotton soil in the rains. One night I dressed up glamorously to go out to Nairobi to sing - high heels and all! I decided to stop in to ask a neighbor at the end of the road if she would like to come with me. It had been raining and it was a dirt road. I did not know what black cotton soil looked like then but within the shortest time had gotten the car firmly stuck. It could not be budged. We had no mobile phones in those days, so I had to get out into the thickly churned up mud, being careful to try to jump from the car to the edge of the road so I did not get stuck too. I walked to the door of our wonderful neighbors and good friends, Mike and Jan McCoy, to ask for help. Mike had decided to go to bed early that night, so even though it was only 7 pm, he already had his pajamas on. But Mike good naturedly put his wellington boots on over his pajamas and helped push me out.

When we finished and I was free from the mud's grip, Mike was covered head to toe in mud thrown up from the tires. Needless to say, my night and my outfit were also totally ruined! We still laugh about it whenever we see them.

I got into singing because Hugh's first job teaching at the Banda School didn't pay enough for our family's needs, so I was always trying to supplement our income. In addition to my part-time job as Assistant to the Africa Director of Intermediate Technology Development Group and a part time-teaching job at the Banda School, which provided us with an *Askari* (night guard) for needed protection rather than money, I looked at what skills I had that I might be able to use to gain much needed additional income. Providing for our children was a constant stress and worry for us under these circumstances. Our working terms were similar to those of Peace Corps volunteers, yet we worked at a private school for children of diplomats, Kenyan government officials, successful expatriate bankers, architects, etc. Consequently, we were aware of the huge disparity between us and the non-teaching expatriate community. To their credit, most of the parents valued the contributions we were making to the lives of their children. So, they included us in their circle of friends, and in many of the interesting and exciting things they were doing. It didn't seem to matter to them that we were barely holding things together financially. Many of these parents were extremely wealthy and successful people. Some had their own aircraft, a few owned islands, etc. For us, everyday existence was hand to mouth survival. This financial need led me to take on many jobs - or to create them if I couldn't find any. Many of these jobs provided extraordinary opportunities for me, which gave me a full, exciting, and fulfilling life, meeting fascinating people, gaining new skills and experiences. I researched and wrote for the FODOR guide to Kenya; wrote up fascinating memoirs of early pioneer settlers whose lives had been extreme undertakings. These people were so amazing and, though older, remembered vividly many details of their early days in Kenya.

One skill I thought I might be able to use professionally was my singing. I had started singing in front of audiences when I was five years old. At sixteen, I sang in front of crowds as large as 5,000 people and had made a record which played on the radio. Later, I sang with a band in England.

Then, in 1979, before we moved to Kenya, I was selected and trained as a dancer by Garth Fagan in the Bottom of the Bucket Dance Troop – a contemporary/African American dance company. Bottom of the Bucket later changed its name to the Garth Fagan dance troop. Garth Fagan went on to do the choreography for the *Lion King* in his later years. The dance troop went on to travel the world as a professional dance company. I would sometimes go to see their performances in various places over the years after we had returned from Kenya. After the shows, I would catch up with old members of the company that I had danced with. Most recently we had the pleasure of taking our little two-and-a-half-year-old granddaughter to see them perform at ArtScape in Baltimore. She has not stopped repeating their moves since!

So, with a background in the performing arts, I started looking at singing in Nairobi to earn a living. I went to a musical venue in Nairobi called the Hootenany. Here, I met David Fuglie. He was an American music and French teacher working at Rosslyn Academy. Dave played guitar, mandolin, banjo and several other instruments, and he had a taste for funky old tunes I had never heard of. He knew two American brothers, Andy Benson who played guitar and sang, and Pete Benson, who played drums. Their father was the American Cultural Attaché for the US Embassy in Kenya. His diplomatic privileges meant he could import sound equipment and instruments through diplomatic circles for us to use. Someone knew Colin Graham, a British banker by day who worked for Barclay's Bank in Kenya. At night, he played bass guitar and sang back up. We quickly became the band "Cactus" and started getting gigs, performing around Nairobi and the Block Hotel resorts throughout the country. We played American country rock at the American Ambassador's house in Nairobi for the 4th of July celebrations. We held practices at my house so I didn't have to leave my children. My kids grew up on the knees of musicians, holding guitars in their hands. Dave would tell my son, Zak, it was a good way to meet and interest girls, but Zak was too young to care.

One of our regular engagements was on Sunday evenings at

A poster for The Band Cactus. Front center, Andy Benson. Left to Right, Colin Graham, Dave Fuglie, Kathy Rigby.

Band Cactus posing in front of their plant namesake.
Left to right: Dave Fuglie, Kathy Rigby, Andy Benson and Colin Graham.

the Carnivore Restaurant/disco. It was a swanky, hot, new, very popular place for entertainment and dining. I became known as the vegetarian singer at the Carnivore Restaurant.

During the day Andy and I played as a duet at Nairobi hotels. At night we rocked with the whole band! Journalist Kathy Eldon wrote a column in the Nairobi newspapers and followed all of our performances. There was even a gossip column about Cactus and our band members.

Chris Seex, who started the Carnivore Restaurant, and his friends were often at the Carnivore. I remember when a political figure of the day scooped me up off the stage right during a song, twirled me around the dance floor, and then put me back up on the stage, as if no break had occurred. There was always a lot of fun and merriment with people in Kenya.

The Carnivore went on to be ranked by Restaurant Magazine in 2003 as 47th in their list of the World's Best 50 Restaurants. After one of our regular performances at the Carnivore, Chris asked the band to stay after the restaurant closed to have some drinks with him. *Dawas* (the Swahili word for medicine) were good for whatever ailed you and were the specialty drink of the house. They had a unique taste of honey, lime and secret liqueurs. They certainly tasted like honey going down, but packed a punch that caught you off guard. Several hours later when we stumbled off to our vehicles, I watched all the guys drive away, only to discover that my car battery would not start. Lights in the restaurant had gone off as soon as we left. There was nothing I could do but sleep the rest of the night in the car. Even there, outside of the restaurant, lions and other wild animals could come around late in the night. More worrisome was the thought of a roving night-time gang finding me in my car. In the early dawn, I awoke to a crowd of Kenyan workers walking to their jobs. They surrounded my car and gave me a push start that finally got the car started. We all laughed about it. When I finally got home, Hugh never said a word nor wondered where I had been. He hadn't even noticed I didn't make it home that night! He'd been sleeping soundly. I had to get the kids ready for school as normal and go about my day as if I had had a good nights' sleep too.

Block Hotels later paid for my work permit which allowed me to work for them as a solo artist. Such a work permit would have been very expensive and very hard to obtain without their connections and wealth. They also asked me to perform solo at their exclusive night club – the Bacchus Club - in downtown Nairobi. I was the headliner there every night for one solid month, twice a year. I loved it!

Eventually, Cactus disbanded as various band members left the country. I went on to perform with local bands at all of the Block Hotel resorts around the country - their Kenya coastal resorts too. They flew me around in a small private plane. On one occasion, I sang for Stephanie Powers and Robert Wagner at William Holden's Mount Kenya Safari Lodge. Another time, I was accompanied by a fashion show.

Life was grand and I was having the greatest time! Kenya was packed with friends and fun for me in those days. Although the crowd changed daily, going into Nairobi was like a big party, full of young, beautiful people all meeting up day after day. Everybody knew everybody. The New Stanley Hotel Thorn Tree café, in the center of town, was a mecca for those young trendy, adventurous,

Kathy singing at Mt. Kenya Safari Club.

Kathy eating with one of the fashion models and Sara Abakutsa, an upcoming Kenyan singer at the Mt. Kenya Safari Club

highly educated, eccentric, humorous and daring lovers of nature, wildlife, and wild places, as well as city life. Our Cactus posters advertising upcoming engagements hung there. Although the famous Long Bar no longer existed, as in the days of hunting safaris, the New Stanley remained a big draw. One never knew who one would run into, as friends converged in the city center when they came in from the wildest, most isolated areas where they lived. For me, the fun never seemed to end. I could meet up with friends, get advice for band posters, public relations, spots for gigs, and photo shoots while catching up on everyone's latest news and safaris. I would find out who was having the next party, what other bands were up to and where they were playing, and find out what was going on with a huge circle of friends. Few people had telephones in their homes and cell phones had not been invented yet, but the bush telegraph was a very thorough and efficient means of communication. News traveled fast. Life was very sociable with lots of dinner parties and private get-togethers.

Kathy singing as solo headliner artist at the Bacchus Club, Nairobi. (Photo courtesy of George McBean)

Burning the Banda Fields by Zachary Rigby

It was a weekend, not a school day. I always liked using a magnifying glass to look at tiny creatures in the grass. One day, I must have kept the magnifying glass in one spot too long. The grass under my magnifying glass caught on fire! I didn't know what to do, so I just went inside the house without saying a word to anyone. Mom and Dad saw the fire after it really got going and had some pretty big flames, sweeping its way along the ground towards our house. Teachers and workers from the Banda school also saw it and came running to our aid. Luckily, we had running water at that time of year and everyone either put water on the fire, used an old blanket to smother the flames, or stamped it out with their feet. Fortunately, the fire had not spread into the unmowed longer grasses nearby. If it had, it could have been catastrophic, spreading all the way into the Nairobi Game Park, and also burning up houses.

Nairobi Aero Club 1982

After a beautiful safari to Samburu with Heather Alexander and her friends, we were dry and covered in dust, so we stopped at the Aero Club at Wilson Airport for a drink on the outskirts of Nairobi, on our way back home to Langata. The Aero Club was a popular gathering spot at the small airport where tourists, safari groups, farmers, settlers in remote regions, businessmen and 'Kenya Cowboys' came after flying their small bush planes into Nairobi. Because road conditions were often so appallingly bad, small groups of tourists sometimes flew to various game parks from here, too.

Heather and her friends went into the club while I was doing up my sandals and brushing the red earth of Kenya out of my hair in the vehicle. They were already inside as I neared the entrance to the club, when the doors swung open before me, and a handsome, bronzed and fit young man came out. He didn't appear to look at me. But, as we were about to pass each other, without a seconds' hesitation, or any expression on his face to give his intentions away,

Tony Fitzjohn (right) with George Adamson in the bush.
(Photo © William Campbell, used by permission)

this total stranger scooped me up and tipped me over his shoulder. One minute I was on the ground going into the bar, the next he was physically walking away with me. Just when I thought he was going to carry me off to his *manyatta* never to be seen by those who knew me again, he turned around and proceeded to carry me into the bar. This is how I met Tony Fitzjohn, who at the time was assistant to George Adamson – co-author of the famous book and movie *Born Free*. George was the extraordinary man who lived among lions and rehabilitated them back to the wild. Elsa was the pet lioness about whom *Born Free* was written. The book made George and Joy Adamson world famous. At one time Tony was habituating a wild leopard. Like so many, I was completely in awe of their work and supported what they were trying to accomplish with all of my being.

Despite his brief lapse towards cave man behavior (which we all found highly entertaining) Tony was a perfect gentleman. He had earlier starred in a movie where he had played Tarzan. I guess he was still in character when I came along. Within minutes of me being 'kidnapped,' his wonderful English manners and education were abundantly evident. It was all good natured fun. We all had a drink and a lot of laughs around the bar, Kenya-style, before we each went our own way, returning to our separate lives.

I ran into Tony Fitzjohn one more time a year or so later. He invited me to come to Kampi ya Simba (camp of the lions) where he and George Adamson were rehabilitating lions. Then he warned me that there had recently been an incident where a Japanese woman visitor (with a small frame like mine) had been attacked and seriously mauled in their camp. I decided my children needed a mother and declined the invitation, although I greatly admired

The Boyfriend and Other Banda Plays
by Zachary Rigby

Banda school was fun. Our teachers were funny and talented. They liked to play music and put on plays which we enjoyed acting in. I (Zachary) was a red squirrel in a play. I loved being in it. But my sister really had a good time. She had one of the lead roles in a play called *The Boyfriend*. She sang and danced the Charleston, wearing old fashioned clothing. Mom sewed her dress. We all enjoyed going to see her and the play. Rachel has become a star! But it's ok, I really like rugby and am good at playing the game with Mike Evans.

Rachel acting in "The Boyfriend" at Banda School.

Zak playing Rugby. He is to the right of games master Mike Evans.

their work and badly wanted to go. I was a huge fan and would so have loved to meet George. He was one of my heroes. Sadly, I never met him. George was tragically murdered near this camp in an attack by *shifta* bandits.

I never saw Tony again either as he was made to leave Kenya. He carried on his work rehabilitating wild animals in Tanzania.

Chapter Ten
Our 'Kenya Cowboy' Friends

The British Government founded the British East African Protectorate in 1895 and soon after opened the fertile highlands to white settlers. In 1899 the Uganda railway, otherwise known as the Lunatic Express, opened up much of the interior of Kenya to European settlement, and to British pioneers. The building of the Mombasa-Nairobi-Lake Victoria Railway was a 600-mile route that was largely unmapped and barely explored. The entire way bristled with hostile tribes, teemed with lions and breathed malaria. The East African Protectorate became Kenya Colony in 1920 and the country remained part of the British Empire until 12 December 1963, Kenya's Independence Day. In Swahili, it is known as Jamhuri Day – the day Kenya became an independent republic. *(Details from www.britannica.com and wikipedia.com)*

Our new house on Kisembe Estate was located off of the Magadi Road in Langata, sitting on approximately three acres. When we first arrived in the country, I envied people we met who lived in Nairobi or the plush expatriate suburbs like Lavington or Loresho. They were full of people from Europe or America and were much safer areas compared to Langata. But, in fact, we were amazingly lucky that the Banda School was located on the less tamed, not-quite suburban area inhabited mostly by second generation white Kenyans, living spread out on large plots of land, beneath the breathtaking Knuckles of God - the Ngong Hills, as Karen Blixen's farm was. The four rounded hills of the Ngong Hills made them look like knuckles.

Langata, directly beside the Nairobi National Game Park, still had wild animals and the most fascinating second and third generation of settlers, adventurers and explorers. The new friends we made were descendants of early Kenya settlers. They were some of the most interesting and exciting people one could ever meet, full of extreme bravado, knowledge, sophistication and humor, and they

Orphaned Elephants and Rhinos
by Zachary Rigby

Across from our house in the Nairobi Game Park lived the sweetest, most wonderful and enchanting lady. Many of our neighbors kept wild animals for pets, but she had the best pets ever – beautiful, baby elephants and rhinos! Her name was Daphne Sheldrick. Her husband had been a Game Warden with the Kenya National Game Parks. Years before, orphaned baby elephants whose mothers had been killed by poachers for ivory, were brought to Daphne to try to save them. She showed love and compassion for these beautiful, helpless, heart-broken babies who needed her so much. Eventually, after many sad and unsuccessful attempts, she found the recipe for a milk formula that worked and kept them alive. We sometimes visited her and her little ones. She was so warm and loving, you wanted to love her like your Grandmother. She gave me and my sister (and our friends) baby bottles of milk to feed the orphan elephants. We had great fun! We all loved Daphne and her babies and begged our parents to take us over to feed them. They loved the baby elephants, too. Daphne always treated us kindly. She was very patient and kind. We always had to be sure the babies were in their beds in the barn before night time, when the lions would come out, roaming around and looking for dinner. Lions like to eat baby elephants and rhinos.

Rachel, Kathy and Zak with Daphne's orphan elephants. Andrew McNaughton, drummer with the Road Runners, is in the background.

Rachel and a baby rhino with Daphne Shel-drick.

Playtime among friends.

could certainly handle discomfort and danger. No complaining! Their experiences were completely out of normal realms and they were all doing fascinating things. We were extremely fortunate that these wonderful people accepted and welcomed us into their tightly bound community.

One of the first good friends I made after moving to Kenya was Jeni Thompson. She and her family lived within walking distance from our house in the Mews. Zak and I would often walk over to their house and our children would play together in those years before school began. Jeni and Tony's daughter was Tamara. She was tiny and petite with long dark hair, and I think the children conspired to marry later in life.

The Thompson's house fascinated me. They had lived in Africa a long time, and like many African *Wazungu* (whites) they had collected unique and gorgeous things. Tony traveled extensively for his business. He had a beautiful collection of deadly daggers that hung on the wall from many Arab and African countries. We started our own collection of daggers for Zak because Tony's were so splendidly beautiful. The handles on some of Tony's were exquisitely carved and even had jewels set into them. He also collected amazing sea shells, the like of which I have never seen before or since.

On the wall of their home hung a photograph of Jeni holding a lion cub. It captured my imagination and my heart. I loved it. Decades later I asked Jeni about the little cub and she told me that some British army chaps, back when Kenya was still a British Colony, were in the Northwest Frontier District of Kenya around Lake Turkana when they saw a lioness with three cubs cross the road. They very foolishly thought a cub would make a cool mascot for their team. So they snatched the last cub crossing the road and took it home with them, back to Nairobi. They foolishly had not thought about the needs of the cub or the fact that lions grow into large, dangerous animals not suited to city life around people. Soon they found that having a lion cub in the city was against the law. So the Kenya Wildlife Department took the cub and put it in the Nairobi animal orphanage where Tony and Jeni found it. They fell in love with the lonely baby and fussed over him. They talked with the Game Warden, asking how it had come to be there. The Game

Warden saw how the Thompsons loved the cub. He allowed Jeni and Tony to take the cub to their home to look after him until the cub's fate was decided. The Thompsons loved having a lion cub living with them. After about a month, a private zoo in Germany took him. It broke Jeni and Tony's hearts to see the cub be crated for his journey to Germany, but there was nothing they could do about it.

After moving to Kisembe Estate, we became good friends with Julia and Rob Glen, who lived the next road over. Their two children, Kerry and Mark, went to the Banda School with our children and were similar ages. Rob was what we referred to as a 'Kenya Cowboy,' with a Crocodile Dundee knowledge of the natural environment, who made incredible, first rate bronze sculptures of African wildlife and indigenous peoples. He is a world renowned sculptor. Rob used to lead museum expeditions into remote areas and thick African bush. At least one type of bat was named after him, being the first person to discover the species. In his younger day, Rob studied taxidermy in Texas. From this he gained an excellent knowledge of anatomy, which was invaluable to his drawing and sculpting, prior to making the molds. One time, he had an entire dead horse in his studio, suspended from the ceiling. From there, he separated certain body parts, keeping others in their freezer until he dissected them and sketched them in great detail so that he thoroughly understood the way the muscles moved, both separately and together. For eight years, he was working on this sculpture of *Nine Wild Mustangs* for the City of Las Colinas, Texas. There is a museum at the site which shows the processes Rob used in detail. The work itself is a breathtakingly realistic bronze sculpture of the mustangs galloping across a granite stream. We watched Rob work throughout most of the steps of this creation, until he had the molds caste in a foundry in Italy. Rob now lives full time in a Tanzanian game park where he can be among the animals he loves and sculpts.

His wife Julia was a second generation white Kenyan colonial girl with a can-do-anything attitude. She was beautiful, gentle, friendly and kind, with a good sense of humor and adventure. Both of their families originally came from Great Britain and had settled in Kenya several generations earlier. Neither one of them was afraid of anything.

Despite knowing the wilderness thoroughly, and being very at home in a tent, they were also sophisticated, educated, cultured and charming. We were often guests at the elegant dinner parties in their gorgeous home, and relished every one. Rob could keep you entertained all night telling his interesting stories. The Glens kept their own cows. One night shortly after going to bed, they heard a ruckus taking place outside and raced out to see what was going on. Just outside their living room door off the veranda they saw a lioness that had felled one of their cows and was suffocating it by the throat, as lions do. Rob quickly lifted his rifle and dispatched the lioness, standing only a few feet from her. Every time I stood outside of their living room, I could not believe how close to the house the lioness had made the kill. There were lions and leopards around all of our houses far more often than we ever realized.

Our house on Kisembe Estate was even closer to the Nairobi Game Park than theirs, putting us all at risk of a predator's attack — especially the children. Once, the Game Warden came to our house to tell us we should be sure to keep the grass around the house as low

Julia Glen and the kids with the baby elephant outside of the animal orphanage.

as possible – so we would be able to see a lion or leopard stalking us – or even worse, to see the many deadly poisonous snakes that lived and hid in the grass.

It was an astounding thing to meet people who were afraid of nothing. They knew the animals and natural world so well, it was amazing. Their confidence and nerve was incredible. And they seemed to know what to do in every situation.

One evening we hosted a dinner party. We had drinks before dinner in our living room. As I sat across from Rob Glen, who was sitting on the couch with someone either side of him, I saw a cobra's head rise up behind his head. He must have seen the look of amazement and absolute terror on my face. Somehow he knew - he had a second sense about wildlife. I was so utterly shocked, I couldn't get any words out of my mouth. No one else seemed to see it. Not a flicker of acknowledgement registered on Rob's face, but before I could say anything, he had bent forward far enough to pull a knife out from his boot. He quietly bent his knife sideways and quickly put it behind his head, whacking the snake against the wall, cutting its head off, all in one movement. He returned to another sip of his Grant's whiskey (which we kept just for him) without explanation, gesticulation or comment. All in a day's work! Nothing out of the ordinary for Rob.

The Pickford Family

Jill Pickford was a teacher at the Banda School, too. She was married to Martin who was a Paleontologist and Geologist with the Nairobi National Museum. He was also a second generation white Kenyan. They had four very bright little girls. Susie could read at age three. Martin was very often in the 'field' on paleontology excursions. When we would see him, his stories kept us amazed. On weekends we often went into the 'bush' with the Pickfords, bouncing happily along in the Nairobi National Museum's Land Rover, over dirt roads with deep pot holes, hiking through lion country, and climbing extinct volcanos where buffalo lived and had to be avoided. When we stopped for lunch, Martin showed us all of the many bones and signs of animals that our untrained eyes could not find.

During the school holidays we often accompanied their

family on paleontological trips around the country. On our Easter vacation in 1980, we agreed to meet up with their family to stay in the rondavel (a traditional circular African dwelling with a conical thatched roof and a hard earthen floor) where Martin was working far out in Western Kenya. After driving for many hours we had still not found their site and daylight faded. The road was just a dirt track and when we attempted to turn around, we got stuck firmly in the mud. There were no lights and no townships or villages nearby. We spent the night sitting up in the car with our children, who knew where?? In the morning light, the soil had dried out a bit and we got ourselves on the road again. Eventually we found Martin and Jill and spent the next several nights, sleeping all ten of us together, on the hardened mud floor of the African rondavel. There were no hotels or motels with mattresses, so far out in the bush. We spent our days exploring – looking for prehistoric bones, climbing extinct volcanos and reading animal footprints in the soil. Martin assigned each of us a small area to locate bones. When we produced nothing, he very quickly gathered the many bones we had missed and explained what they were. They could be very tiny, million-year-old rodents' teeth.

The topic of snakes always seemed to come up. There were

so many different types of deadly serpents, and everyone seemed to have had a close encounter. Martin shared a story of one of his colleagues who had been working in this geographic location with him. The man saw a tail disappearing into the sugar cane and foolishly decided to grab it for fun. He was all alone. The snake was much larger than he expected and did not seem to wish to be caught. It was an enormous python that fought this threat by wrapping itself around the man's chest and neck. The struggle lasted many hours under the hot tropical sun. Finally, other paleontologists came looking for the man and found him in the tight grip of the python. They helped free him from its certain death grip. He was near exhaustion and death. After killing the snake, they measured it - 18 feet long and as thick as a man's thigh. The paleontologist wore part of the beautiful python skin as a belt and a tribute to his foolish adventure and his close brush with death.

Martin asked me to come to the National Museum of Kenya to take some photographs of him and some of his important paleontological discoveries for an article that was going to be written. He had just returned from working at Lake Turkana on the Abyssinian border for the last four weeks and was brown as a berry. While there, he gave me a wonderful behind-the-scenes tour

Kath examining one of Martin's paleontology finds. Jill, Martin, and Susie Pickford, with Rachel and Zak. As in most cases, Hugh is not in the photograph as he was our photographer.

of the museum's collections, skeletons, skulls of many different animals, Joy Adamson's paintings of Kenyan tribal people, full body skeletons of gorillas and many other unusual things. Martin introduced me to Richard Leakey, the Director of the museum, and son of the famous paleoanthropologist and archaeologist Louis and Mary Leakey, who unlocked several glass doors behind which

Surprise at the Animal Hospital by Zachary Rigby

On the Magadi Road, there was an animal hospital for the wild animals from the Game Park. We were allowed to go in and see some of the animals there. There was a baby elephant there that was not well. The staff let us feed it a bottle. Further back, there were animals in cages that had been captured for one reason or another. Mom went so often that she became friendly with a caged cheetah there. She put fresh water into his drinking bowl and he licked her hand and let her pet him through the bars. One day, the head Game Keeper asked Mom if she would like to see a surprise. He took her to a cage with a tarpaulin over the top. The Game Keeper told Mom where to stand. Then he pulled back the tarpaulin. Instantly, a ferocious leopard jumped against the side of the cage closest to Mom, teeth bared in a snarl. She could clearly see each sharp tooth. Mom, only inches away from the cage, nearly had a heart attack! But the leopard was beautiful.

Kath giving water to the cheetah in its cage at the orphanage.

some of Martin's early hominid discoveries were kept so I could photograph them. I found the experience fascinating and exciting. I fell in love with museums that day.

Andrew and Ann McNaughton were in the last house down our dirt road on Kisembi Estate. Zak often played with their son Alexander. I was friends with Ann, who worked for the Ndugu Society that promoted economic empowerment for vulnerable children. Andrew was an artist, interior designer, and a drummer for the Road Runners, a very popular band with expatriates and white Kenyans alike.

One evening I went to the McNaughton's to pick up Zak. Andrew and I stood outside talking. His dog started barking very persistently near the back side of their house. Andrew went to look. He found a very large puff adder near the side of the house. His dog had puppies

and Zak and Alexander had just been playing with them moments before. One unfortunate puppy had been bitten by the snake. Andrew caught the snake and chopped its head off with a *panga* and draped it over a branch of the tree. It was between five and six feet long, its thick body hanging over each side of the branch. Nightfall was near and it was just starting to get dark as it does in the tropics at 7 pm precisely every night, falling like a curtain from one minute to the next. As the sun bowed low in the sky, it highlighted the snake from behind. It looked very sinister hanging in that tree with the red sunset lighting the sky. The poor puppy died before the night was over. A chorus of frogs sang loudly; the world still turned, unconcerned over the calamity.

The McNaughton house, like ours, was always full of interesting people. I met Marcus Russel there. He, like Andrew, had grown up in Kenya. His father had been a white hunter. One day his father was shot to death by one of his hunting clients by accident, leaving teenage Marcus and his twin brother and mother alone without support. Marcus had spent his childhood in the bush and knew so much about animals and the natural world. He was a seasoned bushman with spell-binding stories. I could have listened to them forever. At a party with friends in the bush, Marcus showed us exactly where to look for scorpions. He could easily pick them up and dispatch of their stingers without getting stung. He now owns Ndolwa House, a small private safari homestead on the south eastern boundary of Tsavo West, and is a professional guide. Marcus knows all there is to know about the wilderness and animals. He knows how to test the wind, how to track, and how to think like the animals he studies and shows to tourists. He was born to do what he is doing and I would unquestioningly trust him with my life in the bush.

Termites

When the rains came and the earth became flooded, flying termites began to swarm. African people would use anything at their disposal – nets, pots or pans – to catch them. They ate termites which they said tasted like butter and were very delicious. It was a joyful celebration with everyone outside trying to catch them. The flying ants were an added bonus of protein provided by *Ngai* (God) free of charge!

One afternoon a young white Kenyan man who had been raised in Kenya was visiting us when he saw a termite walk across our floor. He bolted down onto the floor in a flash and before we knew it, he had picked up the termite and popped it into his mouth, swallowing it. Smacking his lips he said, "Umm, that was delicious!" As he stood to get up, our mouths fell open! We were shocked. We had never seen a white man do this before. To him it was the most natural thing in the world, barely worth commenting on. Why weren't we doing it too? We certainly knew a lot of characters in Kenya who kept us endlessly amazed, amused, delighted and laughing!

Another interesting character was Ernie, the American cowboy. I met Ernie at a party at the Banda School. He came from Arizona. He was a foreman on the Hopcraft Game Ranch on the Athi Plains and he invited several of us to go out to ride the ranch by horseback with him. This was the only way to get around it and to check on things, like being sure no poachers were killing wildlife, or that the fences were not falling down. He had given us directions and we set up a date to go, because there were no telephones to arrange it later. It turned out my friend was not able to go then, so I went alone.

I found a parking area, designed for large groups when they

held polo matches. The house was still so far away I could not see it. I started walking through the grassy savannah. Suddenly, in the middle of nowhere a large cheetah, not very far away, stood looking directly at me. I didn't know what to do. I was far from the car by this point, and the house too. I decided to keep walking. If the cheetah wanted to attack me, there was absolutely nothing I could do about it.

I knew a lot of people in Kenya kept wild animals as pets, but no one had mentioned anything about a cheetah when I was invited, so I wasn't sure if he was wild or not. When I got to the house, I learned that Duma and two other cheetahs had been found when they were cubs. His mother had been killed, so the Hopcrafts raised them from babies. Sadly, the others had not survived. Duma was semi-tame, but he still had a wild side. Duma would lie on the couch inside the living room of the house like a pet dog. When he would spot a gazelle outside the door and was hungry, he would go out and kill it by himself for his dinner.

Ernie took my picture with Duma. He warned me not to hug him though. He had bitten people who had hugged him. He didn't like to be confined and considered arms around his neck as beyond his comfort level. He was so beautiful. I was in love.

Ernie took this photo of Kathy with Duma.

Ironic Twists of Fate

Another amazing family we met in Kenya, Robin and Lucy Needham, worked for CARE, an international humanitarian agency that delivers emergency relief and long-term international development projects. At one point Robin and his family lived in Pakistan. While there, two tiny baby girls were left on their front doorstep. The Needhams adopted them.

Robin worked in such incredibly dangerous countries and in such difficult situations, negotiating between warring parties, riding shotgun on convoys of food and medical supplies meant to reach people who were victims of genocide, through their enemies' territories – in the most extremely dangerous war zones and conflicts. After doing this kind of dangerous work, defying death for 40 years, fate intervened. He was sadly drowned by a tsunami while on vacation in Thailand in 2004. Lucy was also taken out to sea by the giant wave, even knocked unconscious by a log, but she survived.

Our friend Dr. Joe Popp lived in the middle of the Maasai Mara National Game Reserve and worked with dangerous wild animals daily. He walked the reserve, walking into lions, buffalo, and all manner of dangerous animals on foot. The kind of work that Dr.

Joe Popp and his research team, (including me on occasion) did with baboons was dangerous work. He survived an attack by a leopard, he survived the dangerous roads of Kenya. Ironically, Joe died in peaceful and safe upstate New York, USA, in a car accident.

It is hard to understand why another friend, Esmond Bradley Martin, one of the world's leading investigators of the illegal trade in ivory and rhino horn, was murdered last year in Nairobi and not years earlier when his work posed a more direct threat to criminal ivory and rhino horn smuggling networks. It was a risky occupation. Esmond was an American conservationist who had fought against the illegal ivory trade, and the illegal trade in rhinoceros horns for decades.

Chapter Eleven
Fighting Lions with Loo Rolls

One Sunday morning our car would not start, but we still needed to get our weekly supplies from the *duka* (grocery store). Hugh and I decided to make an outing of going to the store by gathering the children, our two dogs, Jaws and Hyena, and our woven shopping baskets. At the end of our quiet Sunday walk across the unpaved roads of the *vlei* (a flat plain) approximately one-and-a-half miles, we walked up a short hill which emptied onto a small housing estate on paved roads where the *duka* was located. We made our purchases and walked slowly back, struggling under the weight of two large over-filled woven shopping baskets on each of our shoulders. Because Hugh and I carried heavy loads, Rachel and Zachary and the dogs were walking quite far ahead of us, but within sight.

We noticed Hyena moving to the side of the road, sticking his nose into tall grass. He suddenly retreated and started running towards the kids. Almost immediately, I saw a snake coiling and striking fast behind him. We started yelling to the children to run towards us and away from the approaching dogs. They didn't seem to hear us. Hyena was rapidly getting nearer to them with the snake in hot pursuit. Fear pounded in my veins. My heart beat so loudly, I could barely hear my voice over its thumping.

Hugh and I ran as fast as we could when we realized what was happening, but it was as if we were in slow motion, unable to stop the unthinkable from occurring, voices screaming into the void. We watched in horror as the snake, intent on striking the dogs, darted between Rachel's legs. Time stood still as my lungs refused to breathe.

My voice seemed to freeze on the air and stay suspended before it evaporated into nothingness. As I ran towards them, I seemed not to move at all. Running towards them, groceries abandoned on the ground, but still too far away, I gasped and prayed for God's help. I felt there could be no happy outcome from this situation. Someone had to be bitten by this intensely aggressive attacking snake. I prayed it would be one of the dogs and not my children. I felt so helpless - there was nothing I could do. The entire scene seemed to be frozen, yet in fast motion at the same time. I had no idea what to do. I did not see any object I could use against the snake. I instinctively wanted to run to my children's sides to protect them — to put my own body between them and the snake.

I was so intent on running to the children that I never even saw the African man who came to our aid. He must have been much closer, but his presence did not even register with me. Somehow, he magically appeared with large stones, a perfect aim, and very quick reactions. He knew just what to do and crushed the serpent with blows from the stones. All I could do was gather my children in my arms, with the greatest sense of relief and gratitude. Amazingly, even the dogs came off unbitten – this time.

We thanked the man profusely for his quick thinking and resourcefulness. In his quiet, humble way, he kept on walking down the dirt road, as if he had done nothing, seen nothing. He did not seem to register what I had felt – that one or both of the children's lives hung in the balance! We owed that kind man everything. Was he real or an apparition? A guardian angel sent in answer to my desperate prayers? The snake was a black mamba and its bite would have meant a certain, swift and very painful death. There were many three legged dogs in Kenya due to snake bites, but none would have survived a bite from a mamba.

Despite that perilous experience, we never tired of the thrill of seeing wild animals in their natural surroundings. Going on safari was the highlight of our lives. My parents had come to visit us from the U.S. They were apprehensive about many of the new things they saw and had heard about from us, but they still wanted to experience what life was like for us in Kenya.

We took them on safari to the Maasai Mara to see the magnificent splendor of the iconic teeming plains filled with animals; the boundless, unspoiled space and wildness where tens of thousands of gazelles, wildebeests and zebras thundered beneath the great, vaulting skies and brilliant sun. Watching them stream across the plains, waves of continuous grunting sounds filled the air together with the see-saw voices of the zebras. Their hides glimmered as they crossed and re-crossed before our car; swishing tails and tossing heads, like a tapestry of animal bodies as far as our eyes could see. This miraculous spectacle never failed to astound us. We could scarcely believe that a place could still exist on this earth where one could be amidst surging masses of unmolested wildlife in their natural, free state. The tensions of human life eased and lifted at the sight of this wonder, never failing to leave us in marveled amazement.

We had rented a camper, which my parents and the children slept in. Hugh and I slept in a tent. In those days you could set up camp along the Sand River, even though there was no official camp site. Our small tent and camper stood alone in miles of wilderness. I knew the Sand River was a place where you often saw lions, from my walking safari days with Dr. Joe Popp and the Harvard Baboon Research Team. Our friends, the Glens often set up camp there too, sleeping on camp beds in the open with nothing but mosquito nets over themselves, like all self-respecting 'Kenya Cowboys' who feared nothing in the world - certainly not lions!

During the night, without the usual warnings of roars or deep guttural grunts, we were awakened by the sound and feel of hot breath on our heads from the other side of our canvas tent. We looked desperately for something to frighten the lions off with, but the only thing we could find inside the tent was loo roll (toilet paper). Of course, loo rolls were useless and no defense at all. We cursed our lack of foresight in not packing a spear or *rungu*, (a knob-headed club) at the very least, for our defense. Having absolutely nothing to defend ourselves with was so alarming that we burst into nervous laughter. We also stood up, putting our hands over our heads to try and make our shadows seem as large as possible and we made the most ferocious noises we could muster. What else could we do? Throwing the toilet paper at them would make little impact and we didn't want to open the zipper of the tent. Somehow, not seeing the lions faces made it less frightening.

To our good fortune, our movement and noises seemed to be enough to do the trick. Things went quiet outside the tent. We waited a long time, listening hard. Then, carefully opening the zipper, we used our flashlights to scour the darkness outside.

Seeing no lions, we ran to the safety of the more solid camper walls. We squeezed inside, waking the others who were fast asleep and blissfully unaware of how close the lions' mouths had been to our heads. We slept on the camper's floor with no pillow or blanket or mattress - not minding it a bit! Who could have imagined how comforting that hard floor felt? We were safe and would not be eaten! We were certainly no Kenya Cowboys and had had quite enough adventure for one night. Solid walls felt wonderful.

All we could imagine was that the lions must have been young and curious, but not too hungry. If they had wanted to get in the tent, the story could have had a very different ending! I was later told there was a group of young male lions whose curiosity and playfulness led them to jump on top of tents - and those sleeping - to the shock and terror of those inside! It was all in a night's fun for the young lions to hear humans screaming and to see them running and scrambling around.

Three By The Sea Beneath The Baobab Tree

The coast at the Indian Ocean is a tropical paradise. Fringed with coconut trees, the beaches of Watamu, Diani, and Malindi defy loveliness with extensive beaches, covered in white, powder soft sand, unspoiled by development, and colored water in varying shades of green and blue. It is soothingly warm. Coral reefs, many of them protected inside marine national parks, shelter much of the coast, providing habitats for a plethora of sea-life. There's enough breeze for sailing and wind-powered adventure sports, but not so much that it's going to blow you away. Coral reefs protect the beach from heavy surf, creating perfect conditions to swim, float or snorkel.

On our first safari to Mombasa, we camped at the staggeringly beautiful Diani Beach. We had driven via Amboseli National Park with its lush springs which elephants waded through as they ate the verdant greenery, and then through Tsavo West where it changed to arid land with wild scrub brush and giant baobabs dotting the landscape. It was the first time we had ever seen the majestic upside down trees known as baobabs. They looked like a plan gone wrong – like God forgot what he was doing when He got half way finished creating them. Tall and thick and naked, they stand firm and imposing. Their branches look like roots waving at the sky with their gnarled fingers. They adorn the Kenya Coastal region like tall, defending sentinels, like the Tree of Life they are.

Baobabs are as old as history itself, some living as long as 3,000 years. They date back before the birth of man and the splitting of the continents – over 200 million years ago. They are the miracle tree which soaks up water when it rains, retaining it in its trunk, to later produce nutrient rich fruit in the dry season when all around is dust bowl dry and arid. The amazing baobab can measure nearly 100 feet high and 164 feet in circumference, providing shelter, food and water for animals and humans. It was humbling indeed to walk beneath them and to stretch as far as you could around the trunk without even coming close to reaching the next person's fingers. The majesty of the baobab is amazing!

In the stone ruins of a medieval Swahili town called Gedi, nominated for UNESCO World Heritage status, is an eerie 13th century historical and archaeological site near the Indian Ocean, where you feel the presence of spirits watching over your shoulders. Located next to the Arabuko Sokoke National forest, the amazing ruins show it was once a global trading center and prosperous civilization. Over everything hangs an ancient and decaying scent of old civilization. What's left of this vanished city is pretty spectacular. In Gedi's former Palace, stands a huge baobab tree, like a watch dog looking over the ruins, in the very middle of an arched passageway. It forms a hauntingly splendid sight. We wish we could talk to it and unravel the secrets of Gedi's demise.

Kath and the kids walking under a mighty baobab tree at the coast in khanga cloths.

Zak standing in the middle opening of the sentinel baobab at the ruins of Gedi.

The Flying Doctors and the Maasai

Our house was always filled with fun and interesting people. Even at 2 am, people would stop in, knowing I was just returning from singing. Andrew McNaughton, who lived just a few houses down our same road, would often be coming home from his musical engagements with the Road Runners at that hour too. He was an interior designer by day and a kick-ass drummer at night. Sometimes his car would be right behind me when I turned onto our road in the early hours of the morning. There was not much other traffic at that time.

Sometimes Heather Alexander and others would be returning from their nights out and would stop in too. We were all young and pushing ourselves to fit in all of the fun, and lively things we were doing - and loved. After the exhilaration of a performance, I often needed time to relax and wind down before I could sleep anyway. Hugh (our family's dependable rock) and the children, having regular schedules, were asleep in their rooms down the hallway.

Through American friends, we had met an American photojournalist from Time/Life Magazine – Bill Campbell. He was based in Nairobi when not on assignment elsewhere in the world, often covering wars. One evening when he was in Kenya and was

Maasai Moran warriors dancing alongside young Maasai women.

visiting our home, he mentioned that he would be doing a Time/Life photoshoot on the Flying Doctors of Kenya as they removed cataracts from the eyes of the Maasai people in the field. Maasai country was far from any towns, or hospitals. Hugh very kindly never resented or denied me having an interesting time, even if he also wanted to go, but could not for practical reasons, so I asked if I could go along. He said we had to leave at 4 am. I usually got home from singing around 2 am, so I did not get much sleep that night, but I slept while Bill drove.

When we arrived, we found nothing going on, and not one person had arrived. Bill got out of the car, set up and just waited – like it was all perfectly normal. I don't even know how he knew where to go since there was no village or any other landmark to distinguish this field in the middle of this valley.

Bill had recently returned from the U.S. and had brought a Walkman – the hot item of the day – back to Kenya with him. He gave it to me to listen to music in the car while he prepared for the photoshoot. I fell asleep with the Walkman on my head. The windows were open and my head was resting on the window ledge. Shortly after, I awoke feeling my hair being tenderly stroked. Through my sleepy haze, I noticed that there were voices around me, but speaking in a language I did not understand.

When I opened my eyes, a group of Maasai *moran* (warriors) were standing around the car door, "petting" my head and marveling at my straight, chestnut colored hair. Maasai *moran* are a magnificent sight to behold - beautiful, proud warriors, wearing only their red *shukas* and colorful beaded jewelry. They wore their

Bill Campbell photographing for Time/ Life Magazine for a feature on the Flying Doctors giving eye treatment to Maasai elders.

long hair braided and covered in the blood-red ochre soil of Kenya, their chests were bare, their backs arrow straight, and their features were highly chiseled. The contrast between the gentle way they stroked my head and the fiercesome, brave reputation they possess as warriors, was striking to me. During the slave trade, because of their ferocious reputation, Maasai settlements were avoided by Arab slave traders, who gave them a wide berth.

I took off the headphones to Bill's Walkman and put it on the head of one of the warriors so he could hear the music and understand what I was doing. He was instantly astounded, saying "Ayeeee," as Kenyans do. The warriors passed the Walkman around to each other and were all absolutely amazed.

I got out of the car in time to see Maasai elders slowly wandering in over the hills. I was astounded, once again, at how very well the bush telegraph worked. Eventually a bench was set up and the Maasai elders sat down on it. The Flying Doctors arrived and removed cataracts from one person after another, working down the line, while the patients sat on a bench. There was no operating theatre or much equipment used in the process. Bill photographed the doctors working, and I photographed Bill photographing them. A beautiful edition of Time/Life Magazine showed it all. I had enjoyed another unusual and exciting day!

Coup Attempt

On Sunday, August 1, 1982, we set out to get into our ancient Volkswagen beetle, which was parked outside of the house, to go to the *duka* (grocery store) for supplies and petrol (gasoline). One of the teachers from the Banda School, Dave Charleston, came running across the playing field, madly waving his arms over his head. He told us there had been a *coup d'état* overnight. He said we were all under curfew now, and we would be shot if we went out on the roads. Only then did we notice the deadly calm and total quiet. No traffic was moving.

At 6 am the Voice of Kenya radio station, now controlled by members of the Kenya Air Force, had announced that the government of Kenya had been overthrown in a coup led by the Air Force, following complaints of wide-spread corruption, a dictatorial government, and a failing economy. No one knew who was now in power, nor who the new leaders of the country would be. Students from the University of Nairobi and Kenyatta University College were being called on to join in the street demonstrations. Other people were told they should remain indoors.

Around 7:30 am, it was announced that the government was in the hands of the People's Redemption Council. By 8 am gunshots were clearly audible above the speaker's voice. Announcements became strained and desperate. Even more gun shots were heard and then the radio went off the air. People began looting throughout the city. Gunfire could be heard loud and steady in Nairobi and Westlands as army forces loyal to President Moi fought to regain control.

Back in Langata, removed from what was happening in downtown Nairobi and Westlands, the silence was eerily frightening. Rachel, our daughter, had spent the night with her friend nearby. We walked there through the tall grass, which we would normally never do, because of the many poisonous snakes that lived there. Even lions could be hidden there. But going out on the road was out of the question as it would have been even more dangerous.

The Pelizzolis greeted us warmly and we stayed for a nice lunch as we all discussed what we should do and how we might be affected. Later we walked over to our great friends, Ann and Andrew McNaughton (the drummer for the Road Runners Band), who lived at the end of the unpaved road that our house was on. We decided to pool our food and weapons. We also decided our house was far too dangerous to stay in because it was near the main Magadi Road and who knew what would unfold during the night.

The McNaughtons had a telephone and I tried to call my parents, thinking they would be worried, but the lines were down. We all spent the night sleeping on the floor, seeking safety in numbers. Everyone was terrified, fearing a blood bath and attacks on the houses would take place at any time.

At 10:30 am the next morning, the Voice of Kenya radio resumed transmission with the statement in Swahili that everything was under control and that President Moi's government was firmly back in power. Pockets of fighting continued and sporadic gunfire from automatic weapons could still be heard from downtown Nairobi. Public anxiety ran high. People who had been caught driving through the city during the coup attempt had been forced to get out of their cars by Air Force personnel with machine guns, and lie on the ground with hands over their heads. The nervous military had fired off shots near the heads of those lying on the ground. People caught in the middle hid in bushes and flower beds, while others, caught in the crossfire, lay dead.

Nairobi and surrounding areas had been heavily looted. The central business district was a ghost town with shattered glass and debris littering the streets. Army and police patrols were posted along the streets with semi-automatic guns at the ready. In some areas, shooting continued and people ran around with their hands up over their heads. Transportation came to a halt. Police and army set up roadblocks and checkpoints throughout the city and surrounding areas. They searched and questioned everyone.

In the weeks following the coup attempt, there were shortages of the most basic food provisions. Lines of people stood outside of *dukas* that were mostly empty - semi-automatic weapons were held on all of us. Only three people were allowed into the store at one time. Once inside, you were lucky to find anything you needed. College campuses were sealed, students were ordered to report to their area chiefs.

After a number of days, things returned to 'normal' with limited transportation back on the road. A trickle of people slowly returned to work. The airport and a few trains started running again. Many stories were told over the next few weeks. Outside the City Morgue and the Kenyatta Hospital mortuary, large queues of anxious relatives were looking for relatives or friends who were missing, believed killed in the attempted coup. People started gathering at the morgue early Friday morning following an announcement on the radio the previous night. After waiting for hours, only four to six people were allowed in at a time. Clothing was sometimes the best way for people to recognize their relatives.

Large patrols of police still combed the city. Fear and speculation of rebel threats continued. Police and army road blocks became a regular feature. Night life in Nairobi came to an end. Barricading oneself in after dark became a way of life. We battened down the hatches like everyone else. My joyous singing life ended. Life as we all had known it was over.

Chapter Twelve
The Worm That Ate Our Dog
and Other Things We Didn't Know

One day we noticed a curious swelling on our dog's back. We decided to watch it. Each day it got larger, but Jaws seemed healthy and energetic enough. Something about the lump looked very peculiar. It grew rapidly and seemed to be moving inside! When it reached the size of a golf ball, we decided to lance it open. An opaque white worm or grub-like creature started to emerge. We pulled and pulled, nearly gagging and shrieking all the while this disgusting aberration made its appearance. How did this grub get under his skin? What was it? The smell was horrible. His flesh was being eaten by this grub.

Our African employee came in while we were in the middle of this process. He knew what it was right away. He called it a mango worm. He said we could get them too if the laundry fell on the ground and then we wore the clothing. It was essential to iron the clothes well with a hot iron before wearing them. The female mango fly or tumbo fly lays its eggs on the ground or onto clothing. When the eggs find a mammal, they burrow into it, penetrating the skin. People will usually complain that their body is itching and within three days, painful, boil-like lesions occur. These lesions can become debilitating and sometimes even fatal as the larvae feed and develop on the host's dead or living tissues.

When we lived in Kenya, there was no google or internet, or Animal Planet from which to get information on these natural phenomena. Of course the African people had a vast amount of accumulated local knowledge of these things. Today I see television programs on parasites of all kinds which we suffered from but knew nothing about.

Eating in Kenya

Finding and getting enough protein and dairy for a family of vegetarians could be a difficult challenge. As Kenya is semi-arid and rainfall cannot be relied on, it was a difficult place to grow things with certainty. Many fruits grew wild, and the city market had a good choice of vegetables from the rainier parts of Kenya, but getting enough milk for a husband with a bleeding ulcer and two growing children who needed the protein could be a difficult and time consuming operation. Many people kept their own cows for milk. Our *dukas* were like the small corner stores that used to exist in the U.S. and England when I was a young child. They carried a small and limited supply of essentials – nothing like the supermarkets of today. The Langata *duka* was just one small room and so limited in basic essentials that a person could usually only get one or two tetra packets of milk (approximately 1 and one half cups in volume) and one loaf of bread, if they were lucky. Because of the limited supply of things in the *duka*, you were only allowed to buy so many packets of milk or bread. There were no choices like whole fat or 2% or reduced fat, and no choices of type of bread either.

One really had to shop daily, and if you were lucky, you could get enough for that one day. We never saw soya products like tofu. Luxury foods, ready-made goods and gourmet were rare and expensive. We had no fast food restaurants. But we could sometimes buy fantastic homemade samosas - our Kenyan equivalent of fast food. When I bought them we ate them immediately for breakfast, as one had to get to the duka early in order to get anything at all. Living was very basic. That began to change in the late 1980s when the Sarit Center was built, near the end of the time we lived in Kenya. Some imported foods started to come into the country, but Sarit Center was a 45 minute drive away in Westlands and we didn't get there very often.

In the drought of 1983 I would drive for long distances to other, more European expatriate suburbs of Nairobi looking for milk. Getting cheese was also difficult, but there was a local cheddar that tasted good when you could get it. I relied on beans and eggs as sources of protein for my family. The dried beans were loaded with small stones that were hard to see, no matter how many times we sorted through them. We broke many teeth on those stones. Beans often had weevils in them, too. We cleaned out what we could see, but then we just had to laugh about it and say they were extra protein and eat the beans anyway! After all, they were cooked and you couldn't see them inside of the beans. For people who ate meat, one could easily get a good meal. The grassy savannas made excellent range lands for cattle to feed on the wild grasses that grew. Conditions were ripe for many animals to forage well. Fish and produce from the ocean were sometimes available too.

My grandparents both emigrated to the U.S. as young adults. My grandfather came from Germany and my grandmother from France. My parents were first generation Americans. They were young when they married and started a family, so they lived with my grandparents until I was about 8 and my brother was about 10. When my parents could afford to buy their own house, we moved out of my grandparents' home, which I found devastating. I hated to leave my beloved grandparents and cousins down the road. My grandparents' neighborhood had a strong European air about it. Only French and German were spoken in my grandparents' home. Katrinka was the name my Grandfather always called me. His sisters still lived in Germany. We knew them through their letters. My Grandmother's family all lived down the road. Three or more generations also lived in that house and I never lacked for someone to play with as my cousins were of similar ages. I could not have had a closer family. When we had a party, we actually had our own band because everybody played an instrument or sang.

I was grateful to my European family who had always made everything we ate from scratch, providing beautiful, high quality foods for us. It was my model. My grandfather even made his own sausages, and my grandmother made her own noodles. Grandmother came from a tiny village of only 12 homes, one patisserie and one boulangerie in rural, agrarian France called Henridorf in Lorraine. The village was surrounded by miles of fields where everything needed by the village was grown.

Even after relocating to the United States, my grandparents lived in a German/French neighborhood of Rochester, N.Y. ,where English was rarely spoken or heard. When I would go out shopping with my grandfather, we would go to the patisserie in their neighborhood and get *kuchen* – a German cake. Once, he took me to a store where there were chickens for sale. He told me to pick one out. I was a child and thought this was going to be my new pet. After making my selection, I watched the butcher quickly stretch its neck out and chop off its head. I was shocked and horrified and cried! It probably contributed to me becoming a vegetarian as a teenager. It certainly was fresh though, and nothing like our supermarket experiences today.

Because of these early do-it-yourself lessons, I had a positive attitude towards making most things we ate from scratch. I had always been adventurous and willing to try new things. This was just one more way to be adventurous. Eating things that grew wild and that nature had provided had been a long time interest of mine. Living in the very remote places we lived, without the convenience of stores nearby, encouraged that kind of knowledge of the natural world too. While living in the Highlands of Scotland before going to Kenya, I would scrape the rocks near the ocean to gather the carrageenan moss that grew on them and make milk puddings out of it, or pick nettles and make nettle soup with barley from that. Or pick rose hips for their high Vitamin C content. I knew all of the natural dyes found in plants and flowers to color the wools and yarns that I made soft sculptures out of too. So, believing in local knowledge, I talked with the Kenyan people when I saw something growing, to ask if it was safe and edible.

Kenyans supplemented their diets with wild vegetables including a spinach-like plant, which we absolutely loved. It was called *sukuma wiki,* which means it pushes the week. Its addition to their diet got the local population through the week. Later collard greens were introduced in Kenya and the greens also received the name *sukuma wiki.* Wild foods provide vitamins and minerals that can be higher strength and may not be in many of the normal foods we eat. Many ancient cultures know this and harvest wild foods and plants. Plants provide the basis for many modern medicines. I have always thought there might be a cure for cancer out there growing wild that has yet to be utilized. I even went out with a native healer into the Impenetrable Forest of Uganda looking at all the medicinal plants that local people used. I later went through the Siskiyou Mountain Range of Northern California with an American Indian healer who pointed out the medicinal plants to me there.

There was a Kei-apple hedge growing behind our kitchen that produced little yellow apple-like fruit. The Africans (my local, go-to

Kath with her hair plaited in rows, African style, in their back yard.

Google of the day for all things Kenyan) knew them to be edible, so I picked a great many and made them into a nice jam. We also ate the sweet yellow fruits of the loquat tree and made them into jam too. I learned to make my own cheese when I could get full fat milk from my friend Julia's cows. Milk was not pasteurized, homogenized, or tested for diseases, but I figured my friends drank it themselves and gave it to their children, so... Besides, that was what was available and it tasted good and fresh. Tetra pack milk was not nice tasting.

Water was always a very valuable commodity, nearly always in short supply, or non-existent. For clean drinking water I had to haul big, heavy jerry cans of water from Nairobi at least once every week as we got very little coming through the pipes in our home. It often did not rain for a month or more. There were two rainy seasons a year if we were truly blessed – the long rains in March and April and the short rains for a few weeks in November and December. From mid-December to March it is hot, dry, rainless weather. If the rains fail, which it did in 1983, the wildlife die like flies and we humans suffer too.

It never failed to amaze me how the ants would come into the house in long, long lines for water. They made lines down from the ceiling to get the water that I put on the house plants. In the kitchen, they marched in lines to the water faucet in the sink. Every time we turned on the tap, it was solid black with ants for the first several minutes, as they were pushed out in front of the water. It was the same in the bath tub. When we flushed the toilet, so many were drowned that the entire bowl was black. Any drop of water left on the countertop very quickly resembled a wildlife watering hole in miniature. The ants surrounded the drop and drank from it exactly the same way the animals do from the watering holes in the game parks. A miniscule drop of water is like a lake to the ants.

Animal food in cans or dried in bags was not available or sold in Kenya. Our cat ate chopped liver, going crossed eyed and crazy over her favorite meal. Our dogs had fresh bits of meat boiled up with *posho* – the corn meal mush that all Kenyans ate regularly. Sadly, it was to be their undoing in the end. *Posho*, also known as *ugali*, is a cornmeal mush that is a staple food of Kenyan people and most often for dogs in Kenya too. It takes on the flavor of whatever it is cooked with. Unfortunately, it could grow a deadly mold that was not easily tasted or smelled. It was called aflatoxin and had no antidote. If you ate it, you were poisoned. When I worked with Intermediate Technology Development Group, we worked to solve the problem when it was found that whole villages had died from aflatoxin poisoning. The simple solution was to raise the grain, peanut or ground nut storage containers off the ground so that the mold did not start to grow.

We had not been home or left the country for five full years. But now because we had proper employment with the U.N., we were able to return home for a vacation. We were going to Portugal to visit Hugh's parents. They had retired in the Algarve, Portugal after living their adult lives in Cheshire, England. When we arrived in the Madrid airport my son suddenly shouted out in astonishment, "Mom, look at all these white people!" I had never stopped to consider how most of his life we had been a few white people living among a mass of black people. I had never realized that our children didn't know that white people existed in large numbers too.

When we finally had that chance to go on home leave, I worried about the cornmeal the dogs would eat in our absence. I bought a number of bags of posho to be consumed while we were away over our two-month break. I asked several of my friends to check on the dogs while we were away.

We even found a house sitter to care for our pets. But in our absence the food became moldy and the dogs consumed aflatoxin and died a painful death. The children had missed the dogs desperately when we were away and they cried for them often. Our hearts fell with sickening understanding when the dogs did not come running up the driveway to meet the car on our return, our faces turned into masks of misery. This was our beautiful, intelligent, sensitive Doberman, Eva, who had nursed and cared for our tiny kitten, and kept a man from robbing our home, and our fiercely protective Jaws, that we had had from our very early days in Kenya. He had survived poisonous snakes, baboons, porcupines and the deadly dog pack behind our house, only to die from his food. It broke our hearts. They were the best dogs we have ever had and we didn't even get to comfort them or say goodbye. Destiny can be so indifferent. Their time was up. It was their day. Despite my best efforts, their fates could not be changed. Death was a common and every day thing in Kenya, but it hurt no less.

Never people to turn away from an animal in need of help, we had an unusual encounter on our way to Meru National Park in Northern Kenya. Hugh was driving and I was asleep. But something woke me just in time to see a tiny little thing in the road in front of the car. I sat bolt upright. We drove right over it. I thought it was a little puppy. I asked Hugh to turn the car around. We stopped and I got out and lifted the puppy from the middle of the road. Our

Zak holding Firestone and some of the other puppies.

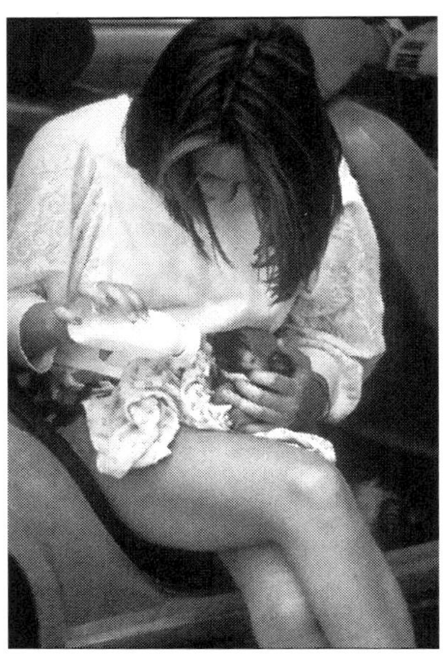

Rachel feeding one of the puppies.

car had gone right over the top of it. It couldn't walk. Hugh said it had been injured. I said it was just too young to walk. I was right. By this time all of the village children had gathered around the car. I told them to bring every puppy they had to me, hoping my efforts might keep their canine population under control in a more humane way. They brought us nine puppies! Ignoring the risk of contracting rabies from the puppies, we now had nine puppies to take on safari with us.

We bought little dolls bottles and milk to feed them. They were enchanting. When we returned to Nairobi, I would drop them off at the KSPCA in the mornings on my way to work. The KSPCA took care of the puppies during the day, and we took care of them at night, until they were big enough to find new homes. Each one of them lived and I found a home for all of them. We kept the original puppy and named him Firestone after the tires that had first driven over the top of him.

Locusts Block the Sun

I was at home near the Banda School on Kisembe Estate when I went in the back of the house to the large vegetable garden where I tried to grow enough food to feed us. I tried to supplement our livelihood by growing our own organic food. I enjoyed watching things grow and thought the health benefits of having no chemicals on our food made the effort worthwhile. I also enjoyed experimenting with different plants to see what grew easily and what did not.

The garden faced many maladies, and it proved to be a formidable task to bring my labors to fruition. Drought was a constant problem. There was usually no running water for our own needs, much less for irrigation. Everything that grew in the garden depended exclusively upon rainfall. I planted a lot of corn because I craved tender American sweet corn. The Kenyans only grew a tough variety of maize. The first time that I tried to grow it, I found that living across from the Nairobi Game Park had its own challenges. The baboons could smell the ripeness of my corn and just about a week before being able to harvest the crop, they trooped across the road and ate every last grain. Thank you very much! In my ignorance, I thought I would tie our most *kali* (ferocious) dog in the corn field to keep them away. Then I learned that baboons love to eat dogs, and they would have been all too happy to make a meal of him.

On this day everything looked normal. As I looked at my plants, I noticed several locusts, and then more came. Within a short time, I heard a loud, unfamiliar noise as millions of wings beat together. The sky grew darker and darker until it was like the black of night, at midday, as a large dark cloud of locusts descended on the landscape. Day turned to night. Millions of locusts covered every leaf of every plant, every tree and every blade of grass. They crawled over my face, hair, body and clothing. I shielded my eyes and mouth as best I could. They gripped on to my hair and skin with tough little claws. I grabbed and pulled, throwing them on the ground by the handfuls. I spat them out of my mouth. I was blinded, having to keep my eyes shut. I wanted to scream and run and freak out, but I couldn't get away from them. Within about an hour my entire vegetable garden was gone, wiped out — as was the rest of the landscape.

Locusts emerge from eggs laid in the ground. They can only crawl for the first six weeks, but they can still cover six miles a day. When they are adults and can fly, they can cover nearly 50 miles a day and eat everything in their path!

I loved the wildness and naturalness of Kenya, which had not yet been bent to the poisons, guns and roads created by man. I decided the price of gardening failure was worth paying just to keep this country as magically untamed by man as it was. Here, the natural and animal world ruled, and I loved it that way. We did, however, have the luxury of buying food that others had grown. I gained a greater appreciation for the struggles that Kenyans faced trying to eke out an impoverished existence on their *shambas* (small plots or farms.) The difficulties in growing food there seemed almost insurmountable, and Kenyans did not have the safety net of being able to buy their food if their crops failed.

Another hazard is Quelea birds that swarm and eat everything in their path, favoring seeds and grains. Forty million of these birds can take five hours to pass overhead. They are nicknamed Locust Birds because they can eat an acre of rice in an hour. Small subsistence farmers suffer the most. One million quelea can consume sixty tons of food in a day.

Chapter Thirteen
A Raider in the Tree Tops

Behind our house, directly outside of our kitchen window, was an enormously large thorn tree covered in the lovely nests of brilliantly colored yellow-and-black weaver birds. These lively mustard-yellow birds were always chirping, making a great cacophony of noise. Weaver birds live in family units or colonies for protection. Their nests are exquisitely beautiful little works of art which have narrow entrances, facing downwards. This helps to protect the nests from aerial predation by other birds. There was always so much happy, busy noise coming from the lively tree, that it was very noticeable when one day the tree went quiet! I had to find out why.

So, I went outside and stood under the tree and stared up. The usual number of adult birds were not present. Squinting up into the sun, I saw nothing for some time, but eventually I saw the rope-like body of a cobra emerge from one nest to stretch itself across to the next. Going from nest to nest, it ate both eggs and chicks. It was using the downward facing entrances to its own advantage. When it finished with one nest, it would extend its long body to the next one, until not a living thing was left. This snake invasion could wipe out the entire generation of offspring for that breeding season. By now a few brave and desperate adult birds returned and mobbed the menacing snake, firing out high-pitched alarm calls and dive-bombing it – to no avail.

The Africans who worked for us often spoke of several cobras they knew that lived on the plot. I shivered to think of this snake running into one of us on the ground, especially one of the kids. I worried often for the children, but most of their lives were spent at the school grounds where the density of humans kept most dangerous elements away.

In addition to Kenya's amazing wildlife, some hazardous like the cobra, I met the most extraordinary people in that country.

The people who came to live in Kenya throughout its history seemed to be a rare breed of an unusual quality. Many were attracted by Kenya's extreme natural beauty, spectacular landscapes of teeming animals, incredible opportunities for adventure, and great vistas of open spaces. Others were drawn to the fabulously untouched beaches and glorious mountains, the endless savannahs and fruitful highlands as well as the great varieties of fascinating African people.

Kenya attracted a cosmopolitan crowd of eccentric and educated wanderers and many artists. They understood the risks of this country of extremes, but were drawn by its alluring challenges and beauty. They shared a fierce love for Kenya's great variety of species, animal and human and aquatic. I thought that living in Kenya was like living in man's natural state –- like our ancestors, among the dangers and excitements of the natural world, surrounded by animals. As soon as I arrived, my fear was replaced by awe. I could breathe, feeling the air and the space and the wind, not cramped or crowded. I felt this was the way mankind was meant to live – as if we were in the Garden of Eden, close to God, with the animals. It was a place of extremes, with great thrills, great fears and huge rushes of adrenaline. Sometimes it was savage, sometimes it was peaceful and harmonious; but it was never dull.

Many who came to Kenya were risk takers– those who wrestle huge pythons alone in remote settings, or walk among lions, buffalos or elephants in the bush, or intrude the crocodiles domain swimming near their lairs. There were those who faced the heavy seas with small ancient *dhows* (Arab boats) or climbed tall mountain peaks or who faced bandits or African soldiers with machine guns. Others dove in shark-infested waters, or wandered dry waterless deserts. Some took great risks to study or film dangerous wild animals, while others braved some of the worst roads in the world to reach their distant destinations. For some, risk is essential. They needed to court danger – or at least the unusual. Many have perished, but to lead a more conventional life without risk was not a life worth considering. For those, with the risk goes the reward; with the fear comes the high. There are those who consider a life of great freedom to be worth any risk at all.

It was our privilege to have known many people like this during our time in Kenya. People whose brave characters and adventurous or entrepreneurial spirits we respected and admired.

Bill Macgill was one such person. As a young man from Scotland, he started taking people overland in a truck from the UK, through North Africa, to Kenya. He often had to deal with extreme emergency situations. Corrupt border guards or government officials or check point delegates wanting large bribes were a common problem. On one occasion a person fell out of the truck and died. Others got sick on his trips and some of them died. Sometimes he travelled through countries where civil war and unrest had just broken out, endangering him and his passengers and trapping them in the war zones. Bill had to do a lot of quick thinking, negotiating, and problem solving to keep people happy and satisfied, to keep people safe, to get them to their destinations on time, and to keep his schedule of upcoming safaris on time.

Despite extreme difficulties, thanks to Bill's shrewd mind, calm personality, and deep understanding of African ways, his safari company grew and prospered. Before he sold his safari company, it had gone from a rough overlander experience for the young without much money, to a luxury safari which U.S. Senators and Congressional Representatives chose to utilize. In true Bill fashion, he learned to fly his own airplane and would on occasion pick up a special delicacy or drink in Nairobi that was favored by a client and fly it to wherever they were on safari in the country, staying on top of his client's needs.

When he and his family eventually returned to the U.K., he built a boat himself in his backyard that he has sailed around the Mediterranean ever since. He also personally built a large home overlooking a lake that he and his son would wind surf on. He bought and owned an entire fleet of aircraft that he leased out, in addition to doing currency and commodity exchanges. He was a very capable and savvy businessman, but he took a lot of risk.

His wife, Liz, was born in East Germany. She said that when she was a child, children were encouraged to spy on their parents and to report them if they said anything against the government. As citizens of East Germany they were forbidden to leave the country. Liz could not live like that, so she attempted to escape the country. She made it across the mine field, but got shot while climbing over the wall. She was put in the hospital to recover. As soon as she was well enough, she escaped and again made it across the mine field, and this time, got over the wall into West Germany, which became her new home. The West German government provided education for her to become a medical doctor. Later, Liz hitchhiked overland alone to Kenya for a holiday and came on one of Bill's safari tours. She says she fell in love when she saw him. They soon married and had a son. For a while, Liz took some of Bill's safari groups to very wild, remote places, off the beaten path. Later she went back to work as a doctor and became head of the ICU in Nairobi Hospital. When Bill started flying and got an airplane, Liz joined him and soon she was flying her own airplane too.

When they sold the safari company and decided to leave Kenya to return to the U.K., Bill flew them back in their personal airplane. Her postcard read, "…the suction pump in the plane packed up, so we had to come down in Morocco. That's nothing compared with the fire on board over The Central African Republic." Apparently a fire had started in their small plane and they had to make an emergency landing. Liz wrote to us about flying along, touching the tree tops with the bottom of the plane, looking for a place to land while being on fire and breathing in smoke. "We ended up landing on a road in the middle of nowhere, but there were 1,000 onlookers around applauding." They survived the emergency landing on the road, somehow avoiding running into any vehicles. It took several weeks to get a new airplane part to them. Her letter was very funny. Bill's cool composure under duress saved their lives. Liz made it sound like it was not much out of the ordinary – at least not for them.

Other friends we made in Kenya worked for organizations like ActionAid on agricultural endeavors, acquiring extensive knowledge of the Kenyan climate, soil and agriculture, animals etc., training and helping the Kenyan people.

Mark Carwardine, a famous U.K. zoologist, environmentalist, writer, conservationist, BBC presenter, television program host, and widely published wildlife photographer from England, became a friend of ours when he took a job as a speech writer for Dr. Mustafa Tolba at the United Nations Environment Program in Gigiri, Kenya. He has gotten himself into some risky and extraordinary situations by studying and filming great white sharks.

Learning to Build by Zachary Rigby

Mom thought it would be good if I got some skills. Next to the road by our house were *fundis,* carpenters who made furniture or anything you wanted out of wood. One summer Mom asked if I could become an apprentice with them so I could learn about building. I did this for a summer. I felt like a man, I was so proud. I was 11. I've got skills now!

Zak with the woodworking fundis

Dr. Laurence Frank studied hyenas at night in the Maasai Mara. Later he began studying lions there. The work that Laurence still does with hyenas and lions is extremely dangerous, as was the kind of work that Dr. Joe Popp and his research team, including me, did with baboons. But Laurence nearly met his end when he visited the neighbors directly behind our house on Kisembi Estate on the outskirts of Nairobi, not on the savannahs of the Maasai Mara. The neighbors kept a pack of 15 large dogs. When he went to visit their owners, the dogs decided to attack Laurence. He narrowly escaped with his life, by climbing on top of his car. His buttock muscles and tissues were stripped all down his leg. Man's best friend nearly took his life, in a domestic situation, not lions or hyenas on the grassy savannahs. We didn't even know the dogs were there until Laurence had his run in with them. I developed a healthy respect for dogs, bordering on fear, in Kenya.

Another neighbor, Daphne Sheldrick, sustained tremendous physical injuries when she confused a wild elephant with one of the orphans she had saved and raised.

My own husband, Hugh, worked in extremely dangerous war zones in Uganda and Somalia to protect children in war zones with UNICEF. He was often being shot at in this capacity, but continued to do that and similar dangerous work for nearly thirty years too. All of these people were devoted to their interesting work, even though it was dangerous. But they would not have changed what they were doing.

Chapter Fourteen
Peter Beard's Camp

Bill Campbell had been a musician before becoming a photojournalist. He took an interest in the music I was doing and came to some Cactus rehearsals when he was in town. Sometimes some of the members of the band the Road Runners, also came to our rehearsals.

Bill suggested that the Road Runners should ask me to sing with them and join their band. The members of the Road Runners had all grown up in Kenya and had been friends since childhood. Ronnie Andrews was a music producer with CBS; he was also the head of the Road Runners. He was looking for new sounds and bands to produce original African music. He promoted the distinctive sound of Lingala musicians from Zaire, with their upbeat rhythms and interesting beat. The Road Runners did not want to change their musical style, but Bill was really trying to get them to change and contemporize the music scene in Kenya by including a woman vocalist.

One evening, Bill took me to Peter Beard's camp, while my good husband cared for the children, tired after his long day. The camp was only one street away from where my family and I were living, but it was of a different time and space. Where Mukoma Road ended, a single dirt track led into Peter 's camp. Here, I entered a totally different world from anything I had ever seen or experienced. It was from another era. I had not known it existed.

This still-thick forested compound with acacia trees and the Ngong Hills framing the background is known as Hog Ranch, for the groups of warthogs that visited daily. A mile inside sat the tent encampment where Peter resided – on and off - since 1962. The compound sits high atop a ridge overlooking what was once Karen Blixen's coffee farm. The four distinct hills of the Ngong Hills, folded together like a mystical fist, dominate the view from the campfire.

Peter was a wealthy American photographer, artist, diarist and author of many books on Kenya. His friends included Karen Blixen, Jacqueline Kennedy Onassis, Lee Radziwill, Fleetwood Mac, the Rolling Stones, Andy Warhol, Lauren Hutton and many others. Despite this, he lived simply and rough – in dangerous, remote areas without any luxuries at all. In keeping with this strange double existence of being rich and pampered on one hand and rough and primitive on the other, he was even married to the model Cheryl Tiegs for a time. Many of Peter's famous friends came to stay at his camp.

Peter Beard first came to Kenya in 1955, seeking adventure. He wanted to live life among the wild things. Deeply affected by Karen Blixen's book, **Out of Africa**, it triggered his lifelong obsession with both the author and the country she wrote about. He thought of Africa as being a place where "you could actually live life rather than have your life run by a world where you wake up in the morning to a traffic jam, rush to catch a bus, struggle to get to the office…" (**The Adventures and Misadventures of Peter Beard in Africa**, Jon Bowermaster, 1993)

The Langata neighborhood where we lived on the edge of the Athi Plains, only one road away from Peter's camp, was the unofficial residence of Kenya's 'wildlife gang' - the country's best known wildlife experts, safari guides, professional hunters, writers and filmmakers and photographers. Carl Jung wrote of the Athi Plains, "This was the stillness of the eternal beginning, the world as it had always been." It felt like life as nature intended it to be lived.

Peter had planned that Hog Ranch would become headquarters for writers, filmmakers, and artists coming to Kenya to work on projects promoting the country's importance to the outside world – a kind of artists' colony on the outskirts of Nairobi.

The evening I visited Peter's camp, an MGM movie producer and crew were staying there for the week and Bill wanted to take me over to sing. Peter's Hog Ranch was the 'old Africa' safari-type camp from the days when animals were hunted for trophies, straight out of a scene from Hemingway's novels. It was a tented safari camp with enormous elephant and crocodile skulls and bones strewn about the place that Peter collected in his many travels around the country, especially when writing **The End of the Game**.

Peter's macabre collages and drawings covered the tables and walls of the open tents – images of body parts of animals and other grisly scenes. Elderly Africans (*wazee* in Swahili) and warthogs wandered around the camp. In the darkness by the sputtering fire light, it could be hard to tell what creature was alive and what was a wooden sculpture. It was a mystical and unreal setting in the darkness, evoking thoughts of the old time safaris, carnage, history, the Africa of Karen Blixen's era and **The End of the Game**, the title of one of Peter's most famous books. Those of us there who knew Kenya's wildlife, knew that leopards and lions stealthily stalked us in the darkened edges of the surrounding shadows. We sat around a roaring camp fire and I sang into the still air beneath the blackened silhouettes of the Ngong Hills - the knuckles of *Enkai* (God). I thought of Karen Blixen's famous words: "Does Africa know a song of me?" I hoped Kenya would always remember mine.

I would never have known the magic of this extraordinary, secret place that embodies Kenya's past, had Bill not introduced me to it. I am forever grateful. That night, I was also introduced to the real Kamante from the book and movie *Out of Africa*. He was a boy with a serious infection whose life was saved by Karen Blixen. He later became her cook. He was then a very old man (*mzee*) and has since departed.

In the next day's light, I decided that I should capture Kamante's

Kamante, Karen Blixen's cook, as an old man.

image one more time before he passed away, so I again visited the camp. To my delight, the resulting image became the cover photograph for the book, **My African Existence**, that accompanied a special exhibition at the Karen Blixen Museum in Denmark from October to the end of December in 2004. The photograph also hangs in the Karen Blixen Museum in Karen today, and I feel I was able to capture a piece of Kenya's history with that photograph. I will forever hold the book dear as it is a connection to my beloved land of Kenya, my adopted home.

Chapter Fifteen
Trips to Tanzania and Lamu

Visiting Ngorongoro

It had been a long held desire of ours to visit the iconic Ngorongoro Crater in neighboring Tanzania while we were living in Kenya. However, it was difficult to figure out the logistics of actually doing it. Taking our car into Tanzania required a lot of government red tape. There was no secure place to leave our car at the border of Kenya and Tanzania for fear it would be not be there when we came back. We couldn't find a tour group that went into Tanzania from Kenya then, so we decided to take *matatus* (African public transportation) all the way from Nairobi to Ngorongoro Crater and around Tanzania. African *matatus* are crowded, but they were plentiful on the roads, so we decided to give it a try, with our children. To our amazement, we got into Tanzania and rode around using public transportation quite well.

We arrived at the lodge overlooking the Ngorongoro Crater. We spent our first night there while we figured out a way to get down into the Crater. The sunset was a blazing orange and raspberry color. The game lodge, like others we saw in Tanzania, had been built in a stunning design using local materials. Delightfully charming, but unlike anything we'd ever seen before, many lodges were deliberately built around enormous rocks or very large trees, using them as features at the core of the building. They made me think of something you would see on the Flintstones TV show, but they were gorgeous. I wondered why there weren't buildings using natural features like these all over the world.

The next morning we hired a Land Rover to drive us into the Crater. The road was so extremely steep, but there were no railings on the sides. We had no seat belts (not that they would have helped if the vehicle had plummeted over the edge). Vehicles coming up from the Crater's bottom hugged the inside wall for safety, while those going down were inches from the extreme drop offs on the edges. I remember looking over the edge to the bottom, barely able to breathe. There was evidence of vehicles that had plummeted off the side at the bottom. Once in the bottom of the Crater we looked back up at the steep escarpment walls surrounding us on all sides. It was a unique and beautiful setting. Game was abundant and magical – just like the Maasai Mara on the Kenyan side of the Serengeti Plains.

After Ngorongoro Crater, we managed to get transportation to Olduvai Gorge to see the area where Louis and Mary Leakey had discovered the oldest human footsteps. I'll never forget the setting. It was completely uninhabited, undeveloped, wild and beautiful. There was no museum, or signs, or interpretation. The footprints themselves were remarkably clear. It sent shivers up my spine to think we were walking where our early ancestors had walked. It was very moving.

When we returned to Kenya, we couldn't have been more excited to get a cold Tusker beer for us and a cold Coke for the kids. Tanzania's economy couldn't compare to Kenya's and a lot of basics were not available. The first thing we did in Kenya was to find a good meal. As beautiful as Tanzania was, we couldn't have been more grateful to be back in Kenya and felt as if we had returned to a land of luxury and plenty.

The Jewelry Exchange

Hugh and I decided to visit the island of Lamu on Kenya's

Wildebeest in Ngorongoro Crater, Tanzania.

north coast. We wanted to experience local culture by first hand immersion. It would be a long, uncomfortable trip by public transportation, so we left the kids with Hugh's brother and wife, and caught a local bus from the Mombasa bus terminal, riding it for many hours. It dropped off and picked up people along the way.

In Garissa District near the Tana River, local people boarded the bus with their goats and chickens, baskets of produce, etc. We rode like this in the heat for many miles. The windows were open and the dry, red dust of this very arid region poured in. Having *wazungu* (white) passengers on the bus was as unusual for the regular passengers as it was for us.

Some passengers wore the traditional, black Muslim burqa or hijab, as many people who live in the coastal region of Kenya are Muslims. Other local women wore brightly colored *khangas* wrapped about their bodies, with another wrapped around their heads. Many carried their babies in *khangas*. They wore 10-12 silver-looking bangles on their wrists, which I thought were lovely. Before long we were bartering some of my things for some of those bangles. It was an interesting transaction, considering we could not speak each other's languages. But women understand these things. We have our priorities, after all. We all love fashion and beauty and don't even need words to work it out, when we really want something.

Everyone was happy with the swap. It was a friendship-enhancing experience that helped pass the long hours of boredom

Kathy getting ready to board the bus next to the ferry to Lamu island.

and sweltering heat and dust – and it gave all of us a new look! It also helped to relieve tension. A number of people had been killed on this bus the week before by *shifta* (bandits) who live in this region, which borders Somalia. Because of those murders, several armed guards had been posted on the bus with us.

After wearing my new bangles, my arm would turn black. I later found out the bangles were made of aluminum, not silver. They had been made by melting down old cooking *sufurias* (pots). Over time, the exposure to this aluminum left permanent black areas of skin on my body. These marks still exist to today – decades later.

Chapter Sixteen
Magendo Licenses Kill

Magendo is bribe money. In this case, it means bribing officials to purchase one's driver's license. Signs that said *Magendo* Licenses Kill were commonly seen along the roadside in Kenya. Driving without proper instruction and training produced some very unexpected scenes on the roads. The roads were already extremely dangerous, and often had potholes so enormous that in many cases they were sinkholes with half of the road totally gone. Most roads had no shoulders on the sides. Untrained drivers, extremely old and unmaintained vehicles, as well as wild and domestic animals wandering about on the roads added to the hazardous driving conditions. The many Kenyan drivers who did not adhere to the rules of the road led to some very interesting and amusing (and sometimes not) situations.

At one point in our decade spent in Kenya, my husband and I had to drive across Nairobi every day to get to work on the other side of the city. One morning we saw three Kenyan gentlemen with broad, beaming smiles driving a beautiful brand new SUV at a very high speed. They barreled along, passing us while going downhill. After passing us, while pulling back in, the Toyota Land Cruiser flipped over and wound up on its roof, sliding rapidly

A roadside sign warning that Magendo Licenses Kill.

down the hill, sparks flying. Then, the camber of the road changed and the Land Cruiser flipped back onto its wheels, righting itself. The driver carried on as if nothing had happened! We passed them shortly after and looked in as we passed. They had slowed down. The passengers had no seat belts on, and they wore very funny expressions of shock and embarrassment, but they were still happy because their car was still working and they were alive.

Once while on safari way upcountry, we were driving on an unpaved earthen road far away from everything except a few small villages. It was an exceptionally wide mud road bordered by forests, and we were the only vehicle on it. We four were in our small Volkswagen beetle with the kids in the back seat. After driving some time, we saw a truck in the distance approaching us from the opposite direction. As he got closer, we noticed he got more and more on our side of the road. We laid on the horn and pulled off the side of the road as far as we possibly could, until we were right up against the trees, and stopped. We didn't know what to do – whether to pull to the right side of the road (where he should have been – Kenyans follow the British driving code which is on the left) or to just stay put and hope he would correct himself. We stayed on the far left against the trees. He kept approaching slowly and hit us head on. We never did find out why he had done this, because the driver then got out of the truck and ran away. No one else around us seemed to care at all. People from the nearby village came over to laugh. We were stuck there for hours in the heat of the day with no drinking water, food, or any other amenities for comfort. But we were glad to be alive and uninjured.

Our accident with the truck.

Other memorable sights were rather amusing for those who were not among the injured or worse. On one occasion, there was a large passenger bus at the bottom of the swimming pool of a leading tourist hotel. It was off of the main Uhuru Highway in Nairobi, off of a round-about and at the bottom of a hill. It would have required turning to get around the circle, and braking to slow the bus down to keep the accident from happening.

On another occasion, a car was hanging in a tree top in a ravine off the side of the road. Drivers and passengers in both cases could not have fared at all well.

In 1983, Hugh's mother, Lady Mary Rigby, decided to buy some Premium Bonds in the UK. Her husband, Sir John Rigby, was vehemently opposed to the idea, saying it was a ridiculous waste of money and suggested that she bought stocks instead. Lady Mary carried through with her own wishes and bought the Premium Bonds — they are certificates of ownership that are attached to a weekly lottery. Even though the odds are stacked against winning, it was not long before she had won £200,000. With her winnings she decided to buy her four sons, her husband, and herself a new car.

This gift of a new car could not have been timelier for our family. We had been driving an outrageously ancient and decrepit Volkswagen Beetle. Among some of the things wrong with it were: it was twenty years old; the driver's door had to be held shut manually; there was no back to the driver's seat, so one had to rely on sitting up straight under one's own muscle power; the windshield wipers did not work, so the driver had to hang out of the window in order to see. In Kenya, this state of decaying automobiles was not uncommon.

There was no car manufacturing in Kenya. Now that Hugh had finally been hired as a full time staff member with the U.N., we had the privilege of being able to order a new car from abroad. Peugeots were popular in Kenya at that time, as they were thought to hold up better than most other cars under the extremely rugged road conditions. In due time, we received the much awaited new vehicle — the first new car we had ever owned — after paying the extremely high import duty, which the Kenya government required, together with the shipping from France.

We decided to take it out for its maiden safari to Amboseli

Rachel and Zak Meet a Cobra by Rachel Rigby

One afternoon my brother and I started on one of our regular bicycle rides down the road that ran in front of our house. We came up to the intersection on the roadway. I kept cycling forward as did my brother, who followed behind me. We were ten and seven at the time. All of a sudden a huge cobra came from our left out of a dirt ditch on the side of the road, lifting off the hot dirt road to confront us, face to face.

Its head was close to us, but we could see its tail, a long way off - out in the field. It was wriggling straight towards us, its cape fully extended, tongue darting forward, with intention to bite. Fear took over and I jumped off my bike and made a run back towards where we had come from. Zak was behind me and I grabbed him, running away, hoping to outrun the cobra. Some African children saw the snake and were shouting at it and running it off the road into the ditch with rocks. The rocks changed the cobra's course. It came directly down the middle of the road towards us and then started to move to the right - off to safer ground, into a man-made ditch on the other side of the road. It swayed, side to side, as rocks came whizzing past its raised and deadly head. Finally, once in the ditch and finding some cover, it lowered its hood and made its way up the dirt channel.

Emboldened by the presence of the African children, we made our way to the side of the road to watch the long snake slither away. Zak and I were simply happy to have escaped the deadly creature, but the African children were intent on killing it, and pummeled rocks into the ditch. Some may have hit the snake, but it wasn't long until it slipped out away into the surrounding bushes. Two of the African boys continued into the roadside bush chasing the cobra with stones, but the snake escaped. Disappointed, they returned to our roadside group, where we thanked them all. Zak and I called our bike trip off, returning home to tell our mother of our lucky

National Park. The dirt road that led into the park for many miles was so corrugated from the traffic it received, that it shook our bones. We didn't realize, but it was also ruining our new car. As soon as we actually arrived in the National Park, our brakes stopped working, the right side passenger door fell off and our axle was broken. We could get minimal repairs done at the lodge, but they said we would have to make our way to Mtito Andei where there was a garage with an African *fundi* (mechanic). We were able to get enough repaired to proceed back out of the park again to the main Mombasa Road.

After being on the heavily corrugated, bone rattling road for just a short while, the car broke down again and we sat there on the side of the road. The car had stopped very near a pride of lions that were taking shade under a tree in the extreme heat of the day. We had to keep our eyes peeled against lion attack while trying to again survey the damage. We sat in the sweltering heat of the car, wondering what we would do now. The children were in the back seat - hot and thirsty. We wondered how long we would have to sit here, as no cars had passed by in two hours, when out of the blue who should come along, but the official French Peugeot Safari Rally team! It was like a mirage!

Kenya road conditions are extremely rough, and many major car companies enter their cars in the yearly Safari Rally to prove their endurance and toughness. The winning car is truly made of steel. The Peugeot Safari Rally team were in Kenya supporting their cars in the rally. When we saw them coming, they were racing to the next rally stop to catch up with their car and make any needed repairs so it could complete the next lap of the rally. We hailed them over. Their lead mechanic (therefore one of the best Peugeot mechanics in the world) crawled under the car. All he could say was, "*Je suis finne*! It is finished!"

They told us all we could do was to get to the main Mombasa Road and get the vehicle towed back to Nairobi to a Peugeot dealer. They did as much of a repair as they could do. It enabled us to drive again. We resumed limping along the road at a very slow speed, with all fluids still leaking, holding the door to keep it closed. At last, we reached a small service station on the main Mombasa Road. Someone from the station went to summon the *fundi* (expert mechanic). When the African *fundi* at last arrived and came running over with a small basket of tools in his hand, our hearts sank. We thought there could not be any possible hope of getting the car fixed with just a few simple tools. And where had this man, living far away from any city, learned to fix cars? We rented a room to stay in while the mechanic worked through the night. We thought we might as well let him try. We had no other option. But we wondered how he could possibly do anything without getting new parts, etc. We settled down for a long stay.

In the morning we met up with the *fundi*. He said we were good to go and that everything was *mzuri sana* (very good). He asked for the sum of 100 Kenya shillings (approximately $14 at the time), which we gladly gave him. We didn't think we would even be able to drive the vehicle out of the station, but to our amazement we got out on the road. Holding our breath, and all the while thinking we would break down any moment, we made

The lead Peugeot mechanic for their Safari Rally team looked under our car and concluded: "It is finished."

it all the way back to Nairobi. That repair lasted as long as the car did, and when we sold the car and left the country, that repair was still holding well. That *fundi* was a miracle man who accomplished, with a few simple tools, what the best mechanics in the world could not. I wish we had paid him a lot more.

Chapter Seventeen
Night of the Scorpion

During the school holidays, Hugh and I decided to leave our children with their Uncle Stephen and Aunt Sally while we took a week-long camping safari to Lake Turkana, the NFD (Northern Frontier District) with a local, low-budget overland safari company. Lake Turkana is a very wild, extremely remote, rugged, undeveloped, lava strewn, volcanic area - a long way from Nairobi. For a week we drove all day and would pitch our tents in the evening while a camp cook prepared our evening meals.

Finally we reached our destination on the shores of Lake Turkana, which borders Ethiopia. After dinner, we sat around a campfire and shared our stories while drinking until the early morning hours. I joined my husband in our tent at 1 am and quickly fell asleep. During the night hours, a scratching sound under my pillow awakened me. I sat up, switched on my flashlight, and looked under my pillow. Not seeing anything, I went back to sleep. This happened several times during the night. At one point, after checking and seeing nothing, I plunged both of my arms under my pillow and went back to sleep again.

In the morning after breakfast, when I lifted my pillow in preparation for taking down the tent, I saw what had disturbed my sleep during the night. There had been a scorpion rustling around under my pillow all night! If it had stung me in the face, or anywhere on my body, I would have experienced agonizing pain, possibly even death. There was no hospital within several days drive.

The next day, my husband and several of the men from the safari group decided to take a walk. We came across a group of Turkana women. The Turkana are a large, strong, remarkably fit, and tough people who live in the extremely harsh, dry, lava strewn, and inhospitable terrain.

When the women saw us, they came over. In an instant they all gathered around me and started pinching me EVERYWHERE as hard as they could. It was painful! The men had to make a circle around me and push them away to keep them from hurting me seriously. As we did not speak each other's languages, I never learned why they did this. It mystified me.

The Day Snakes Covered the Earth

It was a day that seemed like any other. The sun was shining, creating a lazy, relaxed atmosphere. In the early afternoon, I went to the front door to look out across the playing fields of the school grounds, across the red murram soil of the road that separated the end of our plot from the beginning of the school fields. What I saw was unlike any sight I had ever seen before.

Everywhere I looked masses of wriggling snakes writhed over each other, covering every inch of the land. It looked like a carpet of snakes. The sight filled me with chills, knowing that most likely they were poisonous puff adder babies.

A car came down the dirt road, leaving a wake of squashed snakes in its path. Hawks swooped and dove to snatch the squashed bodies. It was wondrous in one sense - to see such an extraordinary spectacle. But the knowledge of how many poisonous snakes lived beneath this ground terrified me – especially with our two young children in the house. The swarming or birthing of these snakes

Becoming TV Personalities by Rachel & Zak Rigby

We did not have a television for most of the years we lived in Kenya. But, after our parents became full time employees of the United Nations, we moved closer into Nairobi. Then we got a television. A lady Dad knew asked if we would make a commercial for Golden Morn Cereal. It was lots of fun. It played often on Kenya TV and can still be seen on YouTube.com. First, an African family are shown eating Golden Morn cereal for breakfast, then a *mzungu* (white) family is shown eating Golden Morn cereal for breakfast. Our friends thought it was cool. *Youtube.com Golden Morn Cereal hrigby* took place over several hours that afternoon, amidst the flocks of swooping birds of prey. Then they disappeared – probably finding homes in the numerous holes in the earthen fields around our house. I never saw anything like it again, I am happy to say.

The Army of Ants and the Tortoises

When we left the Banda to work with the U.N., we had to leave the school house we had lived in for a number of years. We moved to Twiga (giraffe) Hill Road, which was still in Langata. Zak kept several tortoises in a pen in the garden on Twiga Hill Road. They had a nice life where they were able to roam around and catch bugs, eat grass and the vegetation we fed them every day. One day they were unlucky enough to find themselves in the approaching path of army ants on the move - *siafu*. Army ants have large jaws with massive pincers and a very strong bite. Each bite draws blood and can tear and remove flesh. When they swarm, anything living thing in their path is devoured within a very short period of time, even animals as large as cows. They are the piranhas of the land.

When Zak went to feed the tortoises this particular Saturday afternoon, he found them being eaten alive by army ants. He ran back to the house to get us. We put on gum boots (Wellingtons) and long trousers to try to stop the *siafu* from going up our legs and biting us, hoping the slippery rubber boots would stop them. We climbed inside the pen to try to save the tortoises. Within seconds, the ants had crossed our hoped-for barriers and in less than a minute our faces, heads and arms were being bitten. Within the few moments it had taken to get our pants and boots on, the ants had already devoured the tortoises and our struggles to remove them from the ant's path had been in vain. Army ants *(siafu)* kill and eat anything in their way, digesting it even as they tear it apart!

I later learned that one of our neighbors had a cow shut in its pen in the barn for the night when *siafu* came. They estimated it took them less than one hour to pick its bones clean. People with babies in cribs had to be careful they did not suffer the same fate when leaving their babies asleep and unattended. It could happen even inside of a house.

The grip of the *siafu's* teeth is so strong that local Maasai people would seek them out if they were cut deeply. Upon finding army ants, they would hold an ant by its body and let it bite the area in need of a suture; then they would pull the ants' body off, leaving the head and jaw embedded. This was the clever use of the natural tendency of *siafu* to bite - they used them as living stitches.

The jaws of these ants can easily break human skin. They have devoured cows, donkeys, horses, even babies. They are extremely aggressive nomadic ants that kill by overwhelming prey with their massive numbers.

Chapter Eighteen
Jamhuri Day Accident

Jamhuri Day is Kenya's Independence Day - when Kenya gained independence from Great Britain in 1963. It is also the date when Kenya was admitted as a Republic into the Commonwealth in 1964. It is a national holiday in Kenya, celebrated on 12 December each year. *Jamhuri* is the Swahili word for republic.'

As teachers, we were given the day off to celebrate this very important day for Kenya. This particular Jamhuri Day would change my life a great deal, but I didn't know it at the time. I felt no sense of foreboding.

A group of friends decided to go on a picnic in the bush. Hugh and I went in our car, Sandy Johnson, a teacher at the Nairobi Academy, drove his motorcycle. Joe Popp, Susie Emmett, and Glynnis Johnson drove together; several other people rode horses. We settled on a remote spot somewhere in the Ngong Hills. During our picnic lunch lions came around, and the horses became spooked. One girl who had come on horseback went to settle her horse down but it reared up, breaking her foot when it landed.

They immediately decided to get her to the hospital in Nairobi by vehicle. Someone had to take the horse home, so I was shunted onto the horse's back. There was no calming the frantic animal, and I was an accomplished rider who had owned and worked with horses quite a bit. We galloped off as the horse set out for home. I was worried about the lions pursuing us. Many horses in Kenya had tell-tale scratch mark scars on their rumps, remaining long after a lion's unsuccessful attack. I was also concerned about falling into one of the many holes created by burrowing animals. If the horse fell, I might be knocked unconscious, lying among deadly predators. We hadn't talked about what I would do after getting the horse back to its home.

I did not know where the horse lived and there had not been time to ask. Chances are I would not have been able to find my way there through the bush in any case. I counted on the horse finding its own way to the place it considered safe and home. It had broken its head gear (tack) in its desperate desire to run away from danger, so I really had no way of controlling where it went. Everything happened so quickly. Here I was, galloping through the bush without knowing where we were going. Were the lions from our picnic site pursuing us? We were going so fast, I could not turn to look. After about 45 minutes, the horse arrived at a barn in a remote setting and walked into a stall with an open door. I assumed this was home. The other horse and rider were nowhere around. I didn't know what had become of them. I stood outside the barn and thought, *Now what? How do I get home?* I had no idea where I was other than somewhere remote in the Ngong Hills.

Hugh had gone to pick up our children from the birthday party they were attending, so he would not be coming to pick me up. I could only hope that someone had thought to make some arrangement to bring me back home. Then I saw Sandy Johnson sitting on his motorcycle waiting for me. I cursed quietly to myself. Earlier that day he had asked me if I wanted to ride to the picnic on his motorcycle. Joe Popp's warning of Sandy's reputation for speed and recklessness played in my mind and I had declined. Now I had no choice. Seeing no other way home, I hesitantly climbed on the back of his bike, saying a prayer for my safe delivery to myself. I was afraid.

Within a very short distance of getting on the bike, I saw a large drop off - a cliff's edge looming in front of the motorcycle. There was no time to scream, "Don't do it!" as he did the unthinkable. He jumped off the edge, into the canyon below. The motorcycle came down first, as it was the heaviest. My arms were pulled away from his waist. Sandy came down into my spot at the back part of the seat. Seconds later I landed, legs still open, straddling the motorcycle, onto the metal luggage rack. I felt an extraordinary pain that nearly caused me to lose consciousness. I was barely conscious or aware of anything the rest of the way back. It was all I could do to get off of the motorcycle when we arrived at my house. I was in a lot of pain, but I said little. I just wanted to get home, where I thought rest in my bed would put me right again.

The next day I knew my injuries were significant and called my doctor. He was in the final stages of leaving the country to return to the U.S. and was not seeing patients, but he agreed to see me as a friend. When I was unable to get up on the table, he lightly pushed on areas where I said I had pain. He hospitalized me immediately. Tests revealed a broken coccyx and other injuries. I remained in the hospital for over a month, bed bound in traction.

During this time, our recent new car, the Peugeot that we had imported from France, purchased with Hugh's mother's lottery winnings, was being dismantled by thieves - inside of the fenced-in parking lot of Nairobi Hospital in broad daylight! The tires had been taken. When I learned this had happened to our car, it was the last straw. The enormity of the whole situation hit me. I cried in my anger and frustration at being immobile and unable to do anything. By now, the professional medical opinion was that in addition to a broken coccyx and substantial muscle and spinal injuries with compression all down the right side, I had a spinal cord injury which might leave me unable to walk or move ever again - quadriplegic for the rest of my life. My biggest concern was the burden I would be to my husband and young family if this came to pass. I never sang again, of course. My singing career was over as I struggled to survive and pull myself back to normalcy from this injury.

We still had no medical insurance as Hugh was still working for the Banda School, and doing contract assignments for UNICEF. Later I was released from the hospital, to lie in bed at home for months looking at the ceiling in a body cast from my chin all the way down to my hips. A neck brace was added when a break was found all the way up at the second vertebra of my neck. My dear friend, the wonderful Julia Glen, often stopped by to see what we needed. So did Patsy Lane who had also been an early neighbor.

Thus started a long recovery period for me. Things got worse for a long time before they began to turn around. Hugh, ever the good man and dear stoic rock of our family, took me to physical therapy every morning before work and brought me home to my bed every lunch time. He never said one word of complaint about how it affected him. We would not have been able to manage if we hadn't had good Kenyan home help. Many weeks were spent having physical therapy as my muscles, particularly on the right side, wasted away. But luck, or grace, again came through in our hour of need. UNICEF rallied to our aid during this dreadful situation, providing Hugh with a full time staff position, steady and real pay, and much desperately needed health insurance – at last! As soon as the hire took place, I was immediately medivacked to the U.S. for medical tests and treatments I could not get in Kenya. The children and I went to stay with my parents in Rochester, N.Y. while I went to hospitals there. Gradually, I was able to walk again.

As soon as I could, I got a job with International Christian Aid in Kenya, working on international famine relief programs in Uganda, Ethiopia and Zaire. It was meaningful work that I loved and derived so much satisfaction from. The job was giving victims of genocide and drought a new chance to live and prosper. I was deeply moved by their tragic circumstances – especially the children who faced death by starvation. I was still wearing my whole body cast like a butterfly's chrysalis, but improvement continued over time. And like a butterfly emerging, I was returning to a healthy, active and normal life once more. I, too, received a second chance – like the victims of genocide and starvation that I was working to help.

Persistence and resilience ultimately played their roles in our lives, as they had done in the days of little hope when our children were battling cancer and meningitis. Eventually life returned to normal and I grew strong and healthy. My recovery was better than expected. Exercising regularly has kept my spine strong with minimal long lasting trouble after the first five years. Buckets of gratitude go out into the universe.

Chapter Nineteen
Hugh and the UN by Hugh Rigby

When we started to meet expatriates who worked for the United Nations (UN) and other agencies, we heard many of them were trying to communicate foreign ideas to African audiences. They needed illustrators who could assist with this cross-cultural communication. So, I dusted off my illustration skills and started getting much better paying contracts. My first assignment was to illustrate building access for the disabled for Andreas Fuglesang at the UN Refugee Agency. Andreas was quite well-known in the field of cross-cultural communication. He had written an influential book, **About Understanding: Ideas and Observations on Cross Cultural Communication**. So this was a good contact for me.

I was then fortunate to meet George McBean at UNICEF. George had co-edited **Illustrations for Development** and was a leader in the field. He gave me a lot of work, promoting child health interventions such as immunization and oral rehydration, and when UNICEF transferred him to Nepal, he helped me take over his job. The UN was not too pleased about this initially because both George and I were British and they felt the British were over-represented in the system. So, I continued to work as a consultant until they realized that the required skill set was not easy to find and eventually hired me as a staff member.

I found my job at UNICEF to be very interesting, and I earned enough to support the family and we finally had health insurance, but I could be away for weeks at a time, with no reliable means of communication, and often in countries that were then extremely dangerous. Some places I went to in Uganda and Somalia required a military escort as they were so lawless and decimated by war.

On a trip to Hargeisa in Somalia in 1983 I took a flight out of Mogadishu to Berbera. The plane seemed more like a bus. One passenger had a goat, another had some chickens, and another had his cooking stove with him. Fortunately, he didn't fire it up on the flight. When I arrived in Berbera, I was supposed to be picked up by two OXFAM employees to take me to Hargeisa. But no one was there to meet me and they never came. It turned out they had hit a camel on the way to meet me, and both had been killed.

This sounds shocking now, but it wasn't so much then. It was a crazy time. Somalia was lawless, with warlords running the country. Roads everywhere in Africa are very dangerous places. I eventually got a ride to Hargeisa from someone. I checked in at the Kalaab in Hargeisa. When I asked for a meal and a drink, I was escorted to a large room with huge curtains at the end, and given a low table and a cushion to sit on the ground. I knew it was an Islamic country, but someone brought me a large bottle of London Dry Gin with a picture of the Tower of London on the label. There were some locals also in the Kalaab restaurant sitting with their own bottles of London Dry Gin. I got up, walked down to the large curtains and drew them, only to find out that, yes, it was the stage of the British Club (Kalaab).

Hugh's personal armed guards in Uganda

In the 1980s it was common to use a slide projector to communicate. In the early days of trying to prevent malaria, I and others would project a slide of an Anopheles mosquito and say this is what we need to look out for. Local African audiences at the village level, unaccustomed then to a magnifying projection system, would rightly say, "Ayee, we don't have mosquitoes that big!" and reject the whole lesson.

As another example, I was given an assignment to introduce oral rehydration therapy to an area in Western Kenya. I found that the Tusker beer bottle was the exact size needed to get the mixture right, so I used that as the right measure. "Get an empty Tusker beer bottle, fill it with water, and add the prescribed amount of sugar and salt." I hadn't realized that some people would later attempt to rehydrate their children with beer, salt and sugar.

I enjoyed working on the U.N. Flag Stamp Program. Starting in 1980, the U.N. Postal Administration (UNPA) has honored each member country with a stamp depicting that nation's flag. The UNPA issued 16 flag stamps a year until 1989. They sold the stamps to collectors for fund raising. As part of their promotional package for Kenya and Uganda stamps, they asked me to identify the best mother and child painting I could find in each country. The mother and child theme was in honor UNICEF's work for mothers and children.

I chose a painting by Ancent Soi, a Maasai artist, for Kenya and one by Jak Katarikawe for Uganda. We greatly admired the work of both artists, but both Kathy and I particularly loved Jak Katarikawe's paintings of elephants. The first one we saw was at the house of the Douglas-Hamiltons, the elephant experts. But Jak Katarikawe had moved on to other subjects.

When I met him to photograph his mother and child painting and get his permission for UNPA to use it, I told him how much I loved his paintings of elephants and I wished he had painted more so that I could have gotten one. He did not respond directly to this, but he clearly decided to grant me my wish.

Shortly afterwards I received a message from him that my painting was ready and to come to where he was staying in downtown Nairobi. I went to his flat in a busy, dusty part of town. He presented me with an amazing painting of elephants, still wet on the canvas.

I wanted to pay him what it was worth but he would only accept enough to cover the cost of paint and canvas. I walked out into the crowded streets worrying about all the dust sticking on the wet oil paint of a masterpiece. I turned it upside down and carried it above my head. It is one of our most treasured possessions. Decades later, I still look at the painting every day and acknowledge that it is an exceptional work by a great talent. Actually it is more than that, but I can't explain it. This is the magic of great art.

I loved being part of the UNICEF team, but UNICEF move their people around, and I was scheduled to be transferred to Uganda at a time when I could not take our family there. It was just too dangerous. Kathy would have had to stay in Nairobi with our son Zak, and our daughter Rachel would have had to go to boarding school in England. As a couple, we were not comfortable with that, so we sadly decided it was time for us to leave both UNICEF and Kenya. We wanted to keep our family together. It was important to us.

Painting UNICEF by Zak Rigby

At one of my Dad's work meetings at the UNICEF Regional Office for Eastern and Southern Africa, the Regional Director raised the issue that something should be done to decorate the entranceway of the building. Dad suggested that kids should paint a mural on it. That is what they did. I had a good time doing this with a group of other children I didn't know. I felt COOL and important and it was so much fun!

Zak and other children painting the mural for the United Nations International Children's Emergency Fund Entranceway in Gigiri.

As we were making this difficult decision, I coincidentally ran into Andreas Fuglesang at the City Market in Nairobi. He said, "Good Luck! Do you think you will enjoy driving a taxi?" He was being realistic. I thought driving a taxi sounded quite interesting. To cut a long story short, I wound up in Washington, DC. I was told there were successful health communication programs at Johns Hopkins University that might appreciate my expertise. I slid my resume under the door at Johns Hopkins SAIC in Washington, DC. After a few weeks I got a positive response from Johns Hopkins University in Baltimore, and I continued my career in international health communication, flying all over the world, even back to Kenya where we had first met expatriates who worked for the United Nations (UN) and other agencies.

Chapter Twenty
Leaving Kenya

When International Christian Aid left Kenya, in time, I got a job with the United Nations Environment Programme in Gigiri. Hugh was also working on the same UN compound.

Wives of United Nations employees had a fairly tight social group even though we lived in different parts of Nairobi and came from every country in the world. Ulla Demmers of Denmark, Maria Diaz of the Philippines and Salima Bouhafa of Morocco were some of my best friends. There was a very sweet lady from Iran in our wives group. Knowing I was looking for a job, she asked me if I thought I could bear working for a large man from the Lebanon who had a reputation as being difficult. An Asian girl who had been working for him had just quit. I said I would try it and see if it would work out. His name was Fayez Rahbani. He was Chief of Security for the United Nations, Gigiri, Kenya. He was large and loud and imposing, with a force of several hundred guards working under him. I knew he had to maintain strict discipline in his ranks, so I didn't think much about it when he would shout. I understood. He had an important role to play for the safety and well-being of the UN staff and their families and important UN visitors such as US President George Herbert Walker Bush.

Fayez and I got along well and we never had a bad day between us. Fayez grew to rely on me. I wrote all of his correspondence as English was not his first language, but he spoke it well, along with 12 other languages. After a short while, he included me in the inner circle and took me to all high level meetings keeping me informed of things going on beneath the surface – like which foreign leaders visiting the compound were the biggest targets or security risks. He also included me in a particularly bad kidnaping and torture of an important UN representative.

I got to do a lot of coordination work between the UN and various embassies with offices in Nairobi. I also met and talked with visiting Heads of State to find out their security risks and to inform them about conditions in Kenya and how to avoid some problems. During this time US President George Herbert Walker Bush visited the UN Compound and I got to meet him.

Before I left Kenya, I was appointed the Acting Deputy Chief of Security. Several years later, Fayez and his wife, Marina came to see us to be sure we were ok and that things were working out for us in the US. It was so nice of them to do. I'll never forget how caring it was. Relationships in Kenya were strong and all of my bosses had been incredibly good to me, seeming to put a lot of faith in my abilities. I treasured their respect.

As Hugh and I now both had jobs on the opposite side of Nairobi, we decided to move to the plusher, more Western neighborhood of Loresho to be closer to work, and to be in a safer neighborhood. However, I found it boring compared to living in Langata. I missed all the colorful characters and friends we had there and the wild nature of the area, especially the wild animals. But it was closer to work.

A wonderful lady who was our friend in UNICEF Somalia, seemed to have everything a person could want. Her father was an Under-Secretary General of the United Nations, she had graduated from Vassar and she had a great and interesting job with the United Nations. I envied her. But one never knows what tomorrow brings.

She had only one child – a daughter. She and her husband and child had just returned from home leave in New York City to Mogadishu, Somalia, where they were posted for several years. On this day, a group of UN employees who were friends decided to go to the Indian Ocean outside of Mogadishu for a picnic on the beach. The sun was shining and deliciously warm. Friends were enjoying being together again after their separation. Some people swam in deep water. Her daughter was in waist-high water holding hands with other children, playing ring-around the-rosies. The joy and laughter of children having fun rang out.

No one saw the shark come into the shallow water, past the swimmers out deep. The shark turned on its side so that its dorsal fin did not show above the water. It attacked our friends' daughter and bit her in half. Other people ran into the water to help, but it was too late. They pulled the little girl's torso up on the beach. Our poor friend watched it happen. She was the only child she and her husband could have. Hugh was working in Somalia then and was the officer in charge that weekend.

As the family had just been in the US, they had bought their X-Mas gifts while there for the upcoming holiday, which they had planned to spend in Somalia. Their daughter's gifts arrived several weeks later.

Some people have such strength and good hearts beyond measure – or words. Our friend's response to this horrible tragedy and great personal loss was to become a vegetarian. She wanted never to cause harm to any living creature. Her loving and gentle response to such loss was extraordinary.

Civil war in Somalia caused many of her other family members to be brutally murdered. She grieved horribly over so much loss, but her incredible spirit kept her determined to do good and to be the best person she could be. In time, she adopted two other little girls. Few people in this world have been such a wonderful example and shining light in my life. Never give up the most important values. Always be good, do good, and be one.

I still wonder how anyone could endure the losses she did. And her response to be even kinder and more loving than she already had been before. Is there a gene for that? If there is, we should all receive it. We love you dear friend.

It was about a year after that tragedy that the Nairobi office of UNICEF was closed and they offered Hugh a posting in Uganda. Even though the violence of the Idi Amin era had just ended, it was still too dangerous for the children and I to accompany him. So we decided to leave UNICEF and Kenya. Our intention was to return to live in England in Hugh's parents' home. They had a home in Portugal and lived there most of the year. But at the time we needed to go there, Hugh's mother became seriously ill and needed to be in England for medical reasons. So, I took the children to stay at my parents' home in Rochester, NY, while Hugh remained in England looking for work. Eventually he joined me in Rochester and shortly after got a job in Baltimore, Maryland with Johns Hopkins University. The next year the children and I joined him in the Baltimore area. Ellicott City, Maryland was our home for many years.

On one of our last trips into Nairobi when we knew we were leaving Kenya, Zak took his jar of small coins along. He had collected them over the decade that we had lived in Africa. He wanted to buy himself something to remember his life in Kenya. On the way to the store, he saw a woman sitting on the pavement. She held a thin baby whose eyes were covered in flies. Zak put his jar of coins on the pavement next to her instead.

Chapter Twenty One
The After Years

"There is pleasure in the pathless woods,
There is rapture on the lonely shore,
There is society, where none intrudes…
I love not Man the less, but Nature more.
- Byron, Childe Harold (1812)

After our departure from Kenya, a large part of our hearts still remained on those vast, undulating plains that pulsated with resplendent, vibrant life, beauty and brilliant abundance, fortitude and resilience. The country could be devastated by the searing sun, heat and fire, and then turn green again overnight following the much sought after rains. These unique lands were filled with thousands upon thousands of wild animals living in a sanctuary of freedom in the unspoiled wilderness, beneath a great, vaulting sky. When the snow began to fall in upstate New York and the wind howled relentlessly, I cried and wished it was 'my' lions I could hear roaring instead. It was a big adjustment.

While again searching for employment in America, we found that Hugh's Kenyan and African work experiences transferred into a career in international public health. Despite Andreas Fuglesang's reasoned warning that he might wind up as taxi driver, Hugh was fortunate enough to gain a senior position in a successful health communication program at the Johns Hopkins University School of Public Health in Baltimore. He continued to travel internationally, often to various African countries. This helped ease his longing for Kenya and the UK – the land of his youth and family. His foreign travels helped him maintain contact with the vibrant life of Africa.

I applied for work with the U.S. State Department and was told that I had the foreign experience that was needed, but not the academic degrees necessary. So, I returned to college at the same time that our children were going. I won full scholarships and fellowships the whole way through. Having lived in different countries, I sought out other cultures, which led me to work in American Indian Policy at the Library of Congress; Indian Head Start with tribes in the Western USA; as Commissioner for the Maryland Commission on Indian Affairs; and finally teaching Anthropology at various colleges in Maryland. I found a number of similarities between the Native American cultures and the African cultures. They seemed to exist in beautiful color! It was striking. They also loved to dance and put a high emphasis on beauty. Their bead work was similar - colorful and gorgeous; they were closer to the natural world, and both looked to the spirits.

Our children both excelled in prestigious universities and were successful in the work world. We had wanted and tried to keep the family together, but it did not work out that way. We are a true international family with one child in England (where all of Hugh's relatives live) and one child in the USA (where all of my relatives live). Still, we are very close and get together as often as we can. Our love for each other stays strong.

Rachel moved abroad after college in the USA. After various travels, she moved to London and has stayed there for many years. She is an international journalist and has just had a lovely baby girl. Zak and his beautiful wife, Bridget, live in Virginia. He is a manager for Rosetta Stone International language school and Bridget works on legal issues in Medicare and Medicaid. They have a darling daughter. We adore being grandparents and visit often. Our children care about and work towards environmental and wildlife conservation and human causes in their free time. We are proud of them.

We have been fortunate to remain in contact with a lot of our old Kenya friends, who mean a great deal to us. All have been very generous with this book, helping me fill in the gaps caused by time. We are so grateful to have such wonderful and caring friends.

While teaching college Anthropology, I used my cultural experiences to improve lessons and make them more interesting. Now, I teach seniors by giving cultural classes to my community. I continue to support the David Sheldrick Wildlife Trust and other wildlife groups that defend wildlife, as the cause will always be dear to my heart. Writing this book has caused me to relive many of those wonderful days. Our years in Kenya played a huge part in our lives. A lot of our attitudes have been formed by our experiences there. I feel we learned a great deal about the world and how to have even more respect for the various people of the world.

We lived and worked in Maryland and Washington D.C. for over twenty years and Durham, North Carolina for seven. We recently retired and moved to Myrtle Beach, South Carolina where we can go to the beautiful Atlantic Ocean any time we wish. The beaches and the skies even remind us of gorgeous Kenya.

When we look back at our lives, we are so proud and grateful to have our amazing family, to have worked in the professions we worked in, and so glad we got to live in Kenya – which was the most exciting time of our lives – personally and professionally.

Made in the USA
Middletown, DE
30 July 2021

45060423R00094